Effecting Positive Change through Ecotourism

This book is designed to show how ecotourism theory can be put into practice by exploring innovation, program applications, and research-supported case studies in ecotourism. The chapters reflect results of applied research focused on socio-economics of community development; the value of considering system-wide approaches to the relationships between communities and natural resources; the intricacies of capacity building and training facilitators in ecotourism; and education through ecotourism experiences. The cumulative impact of the research presented highlights innovative approaches to visitor management, community engagement, and education to critically address the complexities associated with visitation to natural areas and the dependence upon conservation of ecosystems and associated communities.

This book was originally published as a special issue of the *Journal of Ecotourism*.

Kelly S. Bricker is a Professor and Director of Parks, Recreation, and Tourism in the College of Health at the University of Utah, USA. She has research and teaching interests in ecotourism, sense of place, community development, natural resource management, value of nature-based experiences, and the impacts of tourism. She serves on the boards of the Global Sustainable Tourism Council and the Tourism and Protected Area Specialist Group of the IUCN. With partners in OARS, and her husband, she developed an ecotourism operation called Rivers Fiji.

Deborah L. Kerstetter is Professor Emerita of Recreation, Park, and Tourism Management at Pennsylvania State University, USA. She has published more than 100 manuscripts and multiple book chapters. Her research has been recognized through awards from various organizations including the Travel and Tourism Research Association and The Academy of Leisure Sciences.

Effecting Positive Change through Ecotourism

The Future We Want

Edited by
Kelly S. Bricker and Deborah L. Kerstetter

LONDON AND NEW YORK

First published 2019
by Routledge
2 Park Square, Milton Park, Abingdon, Oxon, OX14 4RN, UK

and by Routledge
52 Vanderbilt Avenue, New York, NY 10017, USA

First issued in paperback 2020

Routledge is an imprint of the Taylor & Francis Group, an informa business

© 2019 Taylor & Francis

British Library Cataloguing in Publication Data
A catalogue record for this book is available from the British Library

ISBN 13: 978-0-367-58344-6 (pbk)
ISBN 13: 978-1-138-39013-3 (hbk)

Typeset in Minion Pro
by RefineCatch Limited, Bungay, Suffolk

Publisher's Note
The publisher accepts responsibility for any inconsistencies that may have
arisen during the conversion of this book from journal articles to book chapters,
namely the possible inclusion of journal terminology.

Disclaimer
Every effort has been made to contact copyright holders for their permission to
reprint material in this book. The publishers would be grateful to hear from any
copyright holder who is not here acknowledged and will undertake to rectify
any errors or omissions in future editions of this book.

Contents

Citation Information   vii
Notes on Contributors   ix

Introduction: Effecting positive change – an introduction   1
Kelly S. Bricker and Deborah L. Kerstetter

1. Community development through agroecotourism in Cuba: an application
   of the community capitals framework   3
   Lauren N. Duffy, Carol Kline, Jason R. Swanson, Mechelle Best and
   Hunt McKinnon

2. Ecotourism influence on community needs and the functions of protected
   areas: a systems thinking approach   22
   Moren Tibabo Stone and Gyan P. Nyaupane

3. The role of private sector ecotourism in local socio-economic development
   in southern Africa   47
   Susan Snyman

4. A new model for guide training and transformative outcomes: a case study
   in sustainable marine-wildlife ecotourism   69
   Kaye Walker and Betty Weiler

5. Watching wildlife in Cabo Polonio, Uruguay: tourist control or auto-control?   91
   Carme Tuneu Corral, Diana Szteren and Marcelo H. Cassini

Index   101

Citation Information

The chapters in this book were originally published in the *Journal of Ecotourism*, volume 16, issue 3 (November 2017). When citing this material, please use the original page numbering for each article, as follows:

Introduction
Effecting positive change – an introduction
Kelly S. Bricker and Deborah L. Kerstetter
Journal of Ecotourism, volume 16, issue 3 (November 2017), pp. 201–202

Chapter 1
Community development through agroecotourism in Cuba: an application of the community capitals framework
Lauren N. Duffy, Carol Kline, Jason R. Swanson, Mechelle Best and
Hunt McKinnon
Journal of Ecotourism, volume 16, issue 3 (November 2017), pp. 203–221

Chapter 2
Ecotourism influence on community needs and the functions of protected areas: a systems thinking approach
Moren Tibabo Stone and Gyan P. Nyaupane
Journal of Ecotourism, volume 16, issue 3 (November 2017), pp. 222–246

Chapter 3
The role of private sector ecotourism in local socio-economic development in southern Africa
Susan Snyman
Journal of Ecotourism, volume 16, issue 3 (November 2017), pp. 247–268

Chapter 4
A new model for guide training and transformative outcomes: a case study in sustainable marine-wildlife ecotourism
Kaye Walker and Betty Weiler
Journal of Ecotourism, volume 16, issue 3 (November 2017), pp. 269–290

Chapter 5
Watching wildlife in Cabo Polonio, Uruguay: tourist control or auto-control?
Carme Tuneu Corral, Diana Szteren and Marcelo H. Cassini
Journal of Ecotourism, volume 16, issue 3 (November 2017), pp. 291–299

For any permission-related enquiries please visit:
http://www.tandfonline.com/page/help/permissions

Notes on Contributors

Mechelle Best is an Associate Professor and Department Chair in the Department of Recreation and Tourism Management at California State University – Northridge, USA. Her research interests include 'greening' or environmental management in hospitality and tourism; slavery heritage and how it is used for tourism purposes; ecotourism and nature-based tourism; tourism impacts; and community participation in tourism.

Kelly S. Bricker is a Professor and Director of Parks, Recreation, and Tourism in the College of Health at the University of Utah, USA. She has research and teaching interests in ecotourism, sense of place, community development, natural resource management, value of nature-based experiences, and the impacts of tourism. She serves on the boards of the Global Sustainable Tourism Council and the Tourism and Protected Area Specialist Group of the IUCN. With partners in OARS, and her husband, she developed an ecotourism operation called Rivers Fiji.

Marcelo H. Cassini is an Associate Professor in the Departamento de Ciencias Básicas at the Universidad Nacional de Luján, Argentina; and he is also Principle Investigator and Research Group Director at the Laboratorio de Biología del Comportamiento at the Instituto de Biología y Medicina Experimental, for the National Scientific and Technical Research Council (CONICET), Argentina.

Lauren N. Duffy is an Assistant Professor in the Department of Parks, Recreation, and Tourism Management in the College of Behavioral, Social, and Health Sciences at Clemson University, USA. She has two major research areas that intersect under the umbrella of critical sustainable tourism: tourism planning and development, and critical pedagogy and global learning.

Deborah L. Kerstetter is Professor Emerita of Recreation, Park, and Tourism Management at Pennsylvania State University, USA. She has published more than 100 manuscripts and multiple book chapters. Her research has been recognized through awards from various organizations including the Travel and Tourism Research Association and The Academy of Leisure Sciences.

Carol Kline is an Associate Professor in the Department of Management at Appalachian State University, USA. Her research interests focus broadly on tourism planning and development and tourism sustainability but cover a range of topics such as foodie segmentation, craft beverages, agritourism, animal welfare in tourism, tourism entrepreneurship, niche tourism markets, and tourism impacts to communities.

Hunt McKinnon is an Associate Professor in the Department of Interior Design and Merchandising in the College of Human Ecology at East Carolina University, USA. His teaching areas of interest are professional practice, ethics, building systems and environmental issues, sustainable design, community design, adaptive reuse history of architecture, and interior design.

Gyan P. Nyaupane is a Professor in the School of Community Resources and Development, and the Center for Sustainable Tourism, at Arizona State University, USA. He has research interests in understanding the relationship between tourists and both natural and cultural resources, and how tourism helps to conserve the environment and alleviate poverty.

Susan Snyman is vice-chair of the IUCN WCPA Tourism and Protected Areas Specialist Group, and coordinator of the Communities and Heritage Working Group within this specialist group. She is currently working for the IUCN Eastern and Southern African Regional Office in the Conservation Areas and Species Programme. Prior to this position she worked as Group Sustainability Manager for Wilderness Safaris, a world-renowned African ecotourism operator.

Moren Tibabo Stone is an Ecotourism Research Scholar at Okavango Research Institute at the University of Botswana, Botswana. He is also a Lecturer in the School of Community Resources and Development at Arizona State University, USA. He has teaching and research interests in sustainable tourism development and management, ecotourism, community-based tourism, protected areas conservation, and rural community livelihoods linkages dynamics.

Jason R. Swanson is an Associate Professor of Hospitality Management and Tourism, and the Director of Undergraduate Studies, at the University of Kentucky, USA. He conducts research on community-based tourism development, tourism trade association management, and tourism policy advocacy.

Diana Szteren is a Researcher at the Laboratorio de Zoología Vertebrados in the Departamento de Ecología y Evolución in the Facultad de Ciencias at the Universidad de la República, Uruguay. She conducts research on interactions between sea lions and artisanal fisheries, and tourism; trophic ecology/analysis of stable isotopes in dental collagen of sea lions; and ecological regionalization of sea lion colonies.

Carme Tuneu Corral has been affiliated with the Facultat de Biologia at the Universidad de Barcelona, Spain.

Kaye Walker is a Lecturer in the School of Business and Tourism at Southern Cross University, Australia. Her areas of research and professional expertise include marine wildlife tourism and management; effective interpretation, its conduct, development and assessment; guide development and coaching; sustainable tourism and its role in building community capacity; the Expedition Cruise Industry; and environmental impact management of marine tourism operations.

Betty Weiler is a Professor in the School of Business and Tourism at Southern Cross University, Australia. Within Australia, Betty is particularly well known for her contribution to visitor management and communication in protected areas, zoos and heritage attractions, and, more recently, on research aimed at influencing visitors' on-site and post-visit behavior.

INTRODUCTION

Effecting positive change – an introduction

Kelly S. Bricker and Deborah L. Kerstetter

'The future we want: Effecting positive change through ecotourism' special issue is designed to engage theory to practice through innovation, programmatic application, and knowledge-based case studies. This is reflected in research focused on socio-economics of community development; the value of a systems approach to community and natural resources tourism relationships; and capacity building and training for facilitators of ecotourism (i.e. guides) and education of visitors through experiences. This issue supports the United Nations International Year of Sustainable Tourism Development through critical evaluation of systems approaches and strategies that improve ecotourism's effectiveness in attaining the United Nation's Sustainable Development Goals. It also attempts to document the extent to which ecotourism affects socio-ecological processes.

The contributions within this special issue emphasize the importance of systematic approaches to complex phenomena such as ecotourism. Duffy et al. explore agroecotourism and ecotourism principles by exploring interrelationships between agroecology and sustainable tourism development goals. Using the socialist nation of Cuba as a backdrop, they explore the complementary nature of agroectourism with ecotourism by utilizing the Community Capitals Framework (CCF). Their findings contribute to our understanding of mechanisms that improve health in its broadest sense thereby contributing to the United Nation's Sustainable Development Goals and enhancing our understanding of ecotourism's contribution to them.

Stone and Nyaupane also support CCF by exploring the complex relationship between ecotourism, protected areas, and community livelihoods within Chobe Enclave Conservation Trust. The focus of their research is understanding ecotourism's role in community capital dynamics, which includes decision making, financial benefits, and collaboration amongst tourism stakeholders. Their results reinforce the importance of accounting for the physical, cultural, social, political, economic, and ecological contexts in rural development. They highlight the benefit of using the CCF to reveal ecotourism's influence on community needs and functions of protected areas.

Snyman's contribution to this special issue elucidates the private sector's potential negative and positive impacts to socio-economic development. Through her research in South Africa, Snyman illustrates that while positive impact exist, they can be dependent on several factors, including the benefits enjoyed, which are often linked to direct employment within ecotourism. As a result, how employment is structured becomes a key factor in benefits sustained by the wider community. She also highlights structural components essential to engaging in successful private sector partnerships – which are important in community development and ecotourism.

Direct engagement of ecotourism experience facilitators (i.e. guides) and receivers (i.e. tourists) is critical to securing positive benefits from ecotourism. To ensure positive benefits from ecotourism in the future, Walker and Weiler introduce a model for developing a nationally accredited training program for whale encounters in the South Pacific. They do this by exploring the capacity for a training model to support pro-environmental perceptions of visitors engaged in the ecotourism activity itself. They reflect on the guide's role in ensuring sustainable management of the tourism experience and discuss how to develop 'critically reflective guides' who 'facilitate positive change' through their 'understanding and knowledge regarding ecotourism and the guide's role in its local and global sustainability goals.'

Corral, Szteren, and Cassini's research addresses the need for policies and education that ensure minimal wildlife impacts. While visitors' appreciation and empathy for protecting wildlife exists, they demonstrate the wide spectrum of behaviors that can cause negative impacts and ultimately negate the potential power of ecotourism to assist in conservation efforts. Concomitantly, Arze and Holladay's case study emphasizes the urgent need to increase education and training, which they argue will ensure support for and an increase in conservation. They also highlight the need for collaboration between the public and private sectors on conservation and livelihood management.

As the researchers in this special issue highlight, innovative approaches to visitor management, community engagement, and education must be utilized if ecotourism is to continue to enhance and contribute to conservation, support livelihoods and community needs, and address the complexities of economic development and natural resource conservation. They also recognize that positive change cannot take place without recognizing that ecotourism is dependent upon and a contributor to the ecosystems within which we operate, inclusive of communities (Dustin, Schwab, & Bricker, 2014).

Disclosure statement

No potential conflict of interest was reported by the authors.

Reference

Dustin, D., Schwab, K., & Bricker, K. (2014). Wilderness, biodiversity, and human health. In A. Watson, S. Carver, & Z. Krenova (Comps.), 2014, *Science and stewardship to protect and sustain wilderness values: Tenth World Wilderness Congress symposium* (pp. 169–175); 2013, October 4–10, Salamanca, Spain. Proceedings RMRS-P-000. Fort Collins, CO: U.S. Department of Agriculture, Forest Service, Rocky Mountain Research Station, 2015.

Community development through agroecotourism in Cuba: an application of the community capitals framework

Lauren N. Duffy, Carol Kline, Jason R. Swanson, Mechelle Best and Hunt McKinnon

ABSTRACT

This study explores the relationship between a Cuban organipónico, an urban, organic cooperative farm, and the surrounding community, particularly in regard to increasing agroecotourism. This was examined through the community capitals framework which allows for the use of a systems approach to inventory and analyse assets and wealth stocks within the community. Individual interviews were conducted in the summer of 2013 with members of the farm cooperative to explore the relationship between the farm and the community, and the way tourism to the farm has improved community capitals. Overall, this study demonstrated the ability for agroecotourism to help support goals of food security, beyond acting only as a tool for economic diversification, but also by influencing other community capitals. The study also adds to the literature on agroecotourism, tourism development in socialist contexts, and the way in which tourism can help support and grow sustainable agriculture.

Introduction

Between 1959 and 1989, Cuba went through drastic political, social, and economic changes brought about by the Revolution. Included in this was policy reform in the agricultural industry that moved private land into government control in order to address the inequitable nature of the Cuban economy. In doing so, the industry faced production inefficiencies that resulted in reliance on food imports. With the dissolution of the Soviet Union in 1989, food imports dissolved, fuel shortages prevented the use of farm equipment (e.g. tractors and machinery), animal feed for livestock was limited, and there was a shortage in fertilisers and herbicides that caused agricultural production to drop to disastrously low levels. Cuba entered into an era characterised by food scarcity, famine, and extreme food rationing. Cubans had to transform their agricultural industry to traditional practices based on agroecology, learning how to grow food without fertilisers, pesticides, and machinery (Pérez, 2011). Organipónicos, or urban organic cooperative farms, emerged across Cuba in order to help alleviate food insecurity by bringing production to local farms. Consequently, Cuba has become an international model for agroecological practices and is attracting scientists, educators, farmers, and other agroecotourists. Using the community capitals framework (CCF), this study investigates how increased agroecotourism to a Cuban organipónico has influenced the farm's impact on the local community.

The CCF is a systems approach that focusses on assets, instead of deficits, by 'identifying the assets in each capital (stock), the types of capital invested (flow), the interaction among the capitals, and the resulting impacts across capitals' (Emery & Flora, 2006, p. 20), that are critical to communities so that inter-relationships between them can be explored in a practical way (Callaghan & Colton, 2008). The CCF has been identified as a tool with strong applicability to tourism research because it can examine and evaluate movements, programmes or industry within a community or region (Flint, 2010; Griffin, 2013; Lima & d'Hauteserre, 2011; McGehee, Lee, O'Bannon, & Perdue, 2010; Zahra & McGehee, 2013). Using the CCF as a framework for understanding the relationships between the community, the farm, and tourism activity, can inventory and analyse assets within the community holistically, beyond examining only economic-centred developmental indicators. The implementation of the CCF framework within Cuba provides an analysis that goes beyond the scope of traditional economic-centred agritourism discourse, and further, applies it to a unique sociocultural and geo-political context. In this regard, this study illustrates the usefulness of CCF in analysing the impact of tourism and provides insight to future tourism planning.

Literature review

Agroecology surfaced in the early 1900s, gained traction in the late 1920s and early 1930s, and was firmly established in the literature by the 1960s as concerns related to how landscape systems are increasingly managed. Although agroecology is not associated with any one particular method of farming, it 'has emerged as a scientific approach used to study, diagnose and propose alternative low-input management of agroecosystems' in a way that moves agricultural practices towards sustainability (Altieri, 1989, p. 37). In that regard, it often includes rural development strategies that address social and economic issues (Altieri, 1989), employs interdisciplinary approach (Gliessman, 2012), merges traditional knowledge with modern advances (Gliessman, 2012), and materialises as a social movement (Wezel et al., 2009). In this regard, agroecology has been proposed as a pro-poor growth strategy for marginalised and resource-poor farmers (Altieri, 2002), food security (Altieri, 2002; Dalgaard, Hutchings, & Porter, 2003), natural resource/forestry conservation, and a means to address climate change (Cavaliere, 2010). Renewed interest in agroecology has followed the calls to address the sustainability issues that conventional, industrial agriculture has brought about (Gliessman, 2015).

Agroecotourism is a niche tourist activity that evolved from the discipline of agroecology; agroecotourists travel to learn about the ecological processes of agriculture. Agroecotourism has also been proposed as an economic development strategy for farmers as well as their communities in Costa Rica (Bagdonis, Hand, Larson, Sanborn, & Bruening, 2009), Belarus (Boldak, Rudenko, Pestis, Pestis, & Rudenko, 2009), Italy (Privitera, 2009), Korea (Choo & Jamal, 2009), and Taiwan (Kuo, Chen, & Huang, 2006). Cavaliere (2010) defines agroecotourism as 'a grassroots ecotourism movement where economically profitable community-based initiatives meet sustainable agriculture systems' (p. 33). While the environmental, economic, and social benefits of *agritourism* are documented (Choo & Jamal, 2009; Gao, Barbieri, & Valdivia, 2014), the notion of agroecotourism differs, in that the visitors hold interest in the biodiversity practices of the farm. In their study estimating agritourists' maximum willingness to pay for 'organic farming activities' in Taiwan, Kuo et al. (2006) found that 'eco-organic tourism' may be the optimal activity to link organic agriculture with tourism over four other hypothetical rural tourism scenarios. Based on field work in Nicaragua, Costa Rica, Australia, Peru, Thailand, Tanzania, New Zealand, and the United States, Cavaliere (2010) presents evidence that agroecotourism can 'produce various benefits such as: job creation, education and capacity-building, community involvement, business viability, a more even distribution of revenue streams, sustainable supply chain linkages, habitat restoration, carbon sequestration, and a decrease in agrochemical use' (p. 34). The tenants of ecotourism differ agroecotourism from traditional agritourism, in that agroecotourism incorporates ecotourism principles: it is an activity that is nature-based, focused on learning – particularly about natural resources and human interaction with the resources, is non-consumptive, ethically managed and low impact, locally oriented in its control, benefits and scale, and contributes to conservation (Fennell, 2008). Most farm tourism and agritourism definitions include 'agricultural setting' (i.e. implying a nature-based setting) and 'education'; however, there are other mixed associations with concepts such as entertainment, authenticity, direct and indirect farming activities, hospitality services, outdoor or commercial recreation, and/or merely something done on a farm (e.g. a wedding or music festival) (Arroyo, Barbieri, Rozier, & Rich, 2013). There are also a wide range of farm types that accept visitors from those who use conventional farming techniques to small-scale organic farms, working farms to petting zoos, and those who offer seasonal activities only (e.g. 'haunted' cormaze or harvest festivals). One contribution of this study is to present findings from research conducted in Cuba, a location where agroecology pervades because of practical reasons (Nelson, Scott, Cukier, & Galán, 2009), though Cuban tourism is still dominated by enclave 'sun, sand, and sea' markets.

Post revolution Cuban agriculture

The face of agriculture changed dramatically with the fall of the Soviet Union. When the dissolution began, there was nearly an 80% decrease in the real population income, a deficit that has only since recovered to about a quarter of its 1989 size (Becker, 2011; Pérez, 2011; Pujol, 2011). Particularly devastating times began in August 1990, the beginning of what is known as the 'Special Period in a Time of Peace', when a series of austerity measures and tight rationing were introduced in response to the economic crisis. It is further characterised by extreme scarcities in common goods and services where meeting basic daily needs became a challenge.

Food shortages were perhaps the most daunting aspect during the Special Period; monthly quotas for rationing often did not supply half of the amount of food needed. The reasons for such severe food scarcity and famine that occurred in Cuba can be explained by a couple of key factors. First, because of continued inefficiencies in agricultural production in Cuba, food imports had been vital but dissolved during this time. Second, oil imports from the Soviet Union declined approximately 90% between 1989 and 1992, triggering shortages of the fuel and petroleum products necessary for industrial agriculture (e.g. tractors, harvesters, and any trucks used for distribution of the agricultural products). Third, because animal feed was no longer imported, the production of meat, milk, and eggs was severely restricted. Fourth, and perhaps most importantly, there was a shortage in fertilisers and herbicides that caused agricultural production to drop to disastrously low levels, with particular impact on sugar cane, which was the main cash crop at the time, occupying 90% of the farmland. It is estimated that agricultural production fell 54% between 1989 and 1994 (Copeland, Jolly, & Thompson, 2011).

With industrialised agriculture no longer an option, Cubans had to transform their agricultural practices overnight, learning how to grow food without the use of fertilisers, pesticides, and machinery (Pérez, 2011). This began with personal gardens in city centres, wherever space could be found such as open lots and rooftops. Some of these small urban gardens evolved into agromercados, or free markets, to help alleviate food insecurities by allowing them to sell surplus to their local neighbourhoods (Babb, 2011), and likewise, many eventually turned into formal cooperative organic urban farms, or organipónicos, such as the one in this study. The political framework for community or cooperative arrangements for farming had previously been established (e.g. agricultural production cooperatives and cooperatives of credit and services; Alvarez, 2004). Moreover, the urban context lends itself to address the food desserts while not relying on fuel for transport and distribution. By 2006, new economic reforms under Raul Castro sought to provide greater room for cooperatives to respond to and work with the market more efficiently (Peters, 2012).

In 2011, Cuba still imported an estimated 60–80% of the food needed for its 11 million people, while food imports cost around $1.5 billion in 2010 (Peters, 2012). Nonetheless, the urban cooperative farm model that emerged in response to food insecurities has allowed for local decision-making and immediate response to community food needs in urban areas that had once faced food scarcity and remain necessary in the fight to reduce dependency on imported food.

Cuban tourism

The tourism industry in Cuba has fluctuated through global economic and social changes, as well as suffered the threat of natural disasters like hurricanes. From the 1959 revolution to the 1989 collapse of the Soviet Union, the Cuban government decried international tourism and focused on the socialist agenda, which included nationalising hotels and tourist operations within the country (Sharpley & Knight, 2009). Tourism was not considered a viable economic sector again until the Special Period when the government was compelled under financial pressure to once again receive tourists. From 1995 to 2012, the international tourist arrivals to Cuba grew from 742,000 to 2,815,000 international tourists, an increase of 279% over 17 years. Tourism's direct contribution to Gross Domestic Product from 2015 to 2025 is estimated to grow 4.4% per year (World Travel & Tourism, Council, 2015). Part of this growth is due to the 'warming' of US.–Cuba relations (Davis, 2015). While Cuba has sustained a strong annual influx of tourism from Canada, with over one million Canadians visiting annually (more 40% of all visitors to Cuba; Embassy of Canada to Cuba, 2013), Europe and Central and South America, the loosening of travel restrictions on Americans will no doubt have a direct impact on economic, social, and environmental conditions in Cuba.

Recently, economic reforms have spawned a wave of entrepreneurial activity among Cuban residents who are entering into the private sector, offering new products or expanding traditional ones. Niche forms of tourism are emerging, such as architectural tourism, revolution tourism, dance tourism, as well as *paladars* (private restaurants) and casa *particulares* (bed and breakfast enterprises; Babb, 2011; Peters, 2012). Specifically, the increasing agroecotourism activity is addressed in this study through the lens of the CCF.

Community capitals framework

The CCF is a system for cataloguing and monitoring community assets and resources by recognising the value of marketable and non-marketable assets (i.e. capitals) and the interdependence, interaction, and synergy between the capitals (Flora & Flora, 1993; Flora, Flora, & Gasteyer, 2015). According to the CCF, *capital* can be defined as a resource that individuals and/or the community possess, that can be invested in, to help increase the wealth of a community, or the different types of capitals (stock). This framework situates community resources/assets into one or more of the following categories of capital: *natural, cultural, human, social, political, financial,* and *built capital* (Table 1).

The CCF was developed from field work conducted in the US and Latin America and has since been applied to rural development (Pender, Marré, & Reeder, 2012), agriculture and food systems (Flora & Gillespie, 2009; Pierce & McKay, 2008; Sseguya, Mazur, & Masinde, 2009), and poverty within the context of lesser economically developed countries (Gutierrez-Montes, Emery, & Fernandez-Baca, 2009). Because of its holistic approach, the CCF holds great promise for analysing the full range of assets within rural and urban communities. It moves beyond the conventional economic-centred developmental indicators to a process that can leverage both marketable and non-marketable capitals to achieve greater community development. Gutierrez-Montes (2005) initially introduced the idea of 'spiralling-up' with regard to the community capitals based on the notion that 'success builds on success'. Emery and Flora (2006) explained that it captures the mutually reinforcing manner of the CCF process 'by which assets [gained in one capital area] increase the likelihood that other assets will also be gained [in other capital areas]' (p. 22). This is perhaps best discussed as the reverse idea of Mrydal's (1957) theory of *cumulative causation* that reflects the 'spiralling-down' period that when there is a loss of

Table 1. Community assets within the CCF.

Capital	Description
Natural	Includes the stock of natural resources, beauty, and geography that characterise the community as a place (e.g. air quality, land, landscapes, water features, water quality, biodiversity, scenery, and natural resource protection)
Cultural	Includes the shared worldviews, values, beliefs, meanings, and behaviours that become tangible through heritage, traditions, language, rituals, dress, and food preparation. Also reflects hegemonic forces that privilege dominant groups
Human	Focuses on the knowledge, skills, and competencies of individuals who can be used to foster community development, particularly leadership. Also includes health and well-being, level of creativity, demographics of community members, and intrinsic qualities (e.g. self-esteem, self-efficacy, and respect)
Social	Refers to the connections/network between individuals and the level of trust, norms of reciprocity, and cooperation they maintain. It also reflects the common vision and goals, acceptance of alternative views, and diverse representation within discussions made about the community
Political	Reflects the 'organization, connections, voice, and power as citizens turn shared norms and values into standards that are codified into rules, regulations, and resource distributions that are enforced' (Flora et al., 2015, p. 184). This also includes level of community organisation through the use of government and the ability of government to garner resources for the community
Financial	Refers to the monetary and financial resources that can be directly invested in other forms of capital (e.g. tax, philanthropic donations, grants, contracts, regulatory exemption, loans, and forms of investment)
Built	Includes infrastructure necessary to support community activities such as housing, transportation infrastructure, telecommunications infrastructure and hardware, utilities (e.g. water treatment, sewer, sidewalks), recreation facilities, and community buildings

Source: Adapted from Flora et al. (2015) and Flora, Emery, Fey, and Bregendahl (2005).

any assets, there will likely be further loss in other assets until there is some type of intervention to stop the decline (Emery & Flora, 2006).

Methods

This qualitative study used the CCF to investigate the relationship between an organipónico and the surrounding community, particularly in regard to tourism to the farm as a moderating force. The organipónico under investigation has nearly 200 cooperative members who work on the farm. It has a diversified product offering including vegetables, ornamental and medicinal plants, and value-added food products such as vinegar and spices. It also provides work-shops for local community members and technical assistance to other organic farms on the local, national, and international level. Tourist activity at the orga-nipónico started slowly. Initial marketing was through word of mouth and by domestic tour operators promoting visits to the farm. Approximately 8000 indi-viduals visited the farm in 2012, largely representing North America, Europe, and Latin America markets-of-origin. Roughly 7400 of the visitors made their arrangements through tour operators or travel agents. In 2012, the farm hosted 35 university groups with some staying up to 20 days to do research on the farm.

The primary researcher established a relationship with the farm through a tour operator working in Cuba and subsequently visited the farm several times prior to data collection; for other members of the research team, it was the first visit. The research team consisted of seven faculty members and six graduate students. Data were collected through semi-structured interviews con-ducted during a site visit in July 2013. Questions were translated into Spanish and provided to the key farm contact prior to the visit who also helped with pur-posive sampling of the participants. Participants needed to be workers at the farm as well as residents of the local community, as well as gender, age, and

Table 2. Description of informants.

Informant number	Role at farm
1	Woman: actively involved in day-to-day operations on the farm; had served as head cook preparing meals for the workers for approximately 10 years. She had also worked in the fields and in sales for the farm. Before coming to the farm, she was an engineer in one of the national-level ministries
2	Man: an agronomist in training, and the original founder of the cooperative farm 16 years ago. He is involved in day-to-day operations and administration of the farm, including long-term planning
3	Man: had come to work at farm seven years ago because of his expertise in a relevant field of science. He had worked in various ministries for the government prior to coming to the farm
4	Woman: has been with the farm 14 years and has had many jobs on the farm, including being involved in community outreach and a tour guide for groups who visit the farm. She was the tour guide for the research team
5	Woman: currently does accounting and payroll office for farm; has also been cross-trained to work in other positions

position on the farm to ensure that many distinct perspectives were captured (Patton, 1987). In total, five individuals were interviewed (Table 2) and data were also collected through participant observations during a guided tour of the farm and informal discussion with farm workers. The data were collected in the form of field notes, sketches, photographs, and video by members of the research team.

Interviews lasted between 30 and 60 minutes, and informants received a monetary incentive for their time. Three of the interviews were conducted by a team of 2 interviewers and 1 translator, and 2 additional interviews were conducted in English without the presence of a translator, for a total of 10 interviewers and 2 translators involved in the interview process. In order to increase inter-rater reliability and dependability of the data, a training process for the interviewers and the data coders was used that included practice interviews and group discussion of the interview process. An interview guide was also used to ensure accuracy across interview teams, to ensure that participants answered a very similar set of questions, allowing for comparison between interviews during the analysis stage (Bernard & Ryan, 2010). The interviews were not recorded due to privacy and security reasons; however, interviewers were granted permission to take written notes. A debriefing by each of the interviewer teams was immediately audio-recorded following each interview; the translator also took an active role in the debriefings. The audio tape of the debriefing was transcribed; these, along with hand-written notes from each research team member and a formal report submitted by each team about the interview, served as data sources.

Interview questions focused on the relationships between the farm and community, the farm and tourism, and tourism and community. Questions for the interviews were grouped according to themes: the nature of the farm's relationship with the surrounding community, a profile of the tourists who visit the farm, the tourists' motivations and interests for visiting, how tourists learn of the farm, activities, and educational lessons provided at the farm, what positive and negative impacts tourists have on the farm or the community, and if the recent changes in private enterprise in Cuba affected the farm or tourism on the farm. Moreover, during the interview, a visual aide and explanation of the CCF model was shared with informants (Kline & Oliver, 2015) so that they could comment directly on the impacts to various capitals (Figure 1).

The qualitative data were analysed by research team members through independent analysis, followed by several meetings to discuss agreement in interpretation of findings and organisation of the data. The first round of open coding produced 11 themes agreed upon by the research team. A second round of coding was conducted with pre-determined codes – the community capitals identified in the CCF. Because the CCF suggests that, conceptually, certain community assets/resources may be categorised under multiple domains of capital, simultaneous coding was employed to address the complexity of examining the capitals. Simultaneous coding is a technique that considers the 'confounding

Figure 1. Visual aide of the community capitals used in the interviews.

property of category construction in qualitative inquiry' because data 'cannot always be precisely and discretely bounded' (Saldana, 2009, p. 6). Finally, it should be noted that while dependability and heightened confirmability were sought through good research design, use of an existing conceptual framework, and built in areas for triangulation (e.g. multiple methods and independent analysis of data), caution should be taken in consideration of the findings. The analyses were based on the debriefings from the interviews, which created an added layer of researcher interpretation; however, this methodological issue was kept in mind through the process and in the formation of the findings. Moreover, because of the intercultural and multilingual context within which this study took place, caution should be taken with regard to interpretation that was 'lost in translation' (see Goldstein, 1995).

Findings

Natural capital

The farm builds natural capital for the community in multiple ways: it serves as an oasis of green space within the neighbourhood that includes soviet style apartment complexes (Informant 4); produce grown at the farm goes directly to the community (Informants 1, 2, 3, 4, and 5); and the farm serves as a living lab to teach and demonstrate how the ecosystem and permaculture, or the intentional practice and design of sustainable agriculture systems that works harmoniously with the nature (Holmgren, 2011), work to employees, community members, student interns, children, and tourists (Informants 1, 3, and 4). Prior to becoming a farm, the land was vacant, and overrun with weeds and trash (Informants 2 and 4; farm tour notes). Situated within a suburban neighbourhood, the farm is surrounded by mid-rise concrete buildings representative of Soviet Union era architecture.

The farm has enhanced biodiversity that may not otherwise exist if the land was used for housing or commercial development (Informant 2). Informants emphasised the farming methods and agroecological practices implemented. For example, interviewees mentioned seed-saving techniques, solar panels, humus beds, rain barrels, irrigation systems, integrated pest management, natural fencing, waste management, and chemical-free operations (Informants 1, 2, 3, and 5; farm tour notes). Farm operations also enhanced the area's natural capital by improving soil quality and conserving and water (Informants 1, 2, and 3).

Cultural capital

The co-op members' dedication to the farm's goals manifests in the overall tone, or culture, that influences their daily actions. The organipónico's culture values cooperative members and the community, engendering a constant drive to care for each other (Informants 1, 4, and 5). For example, the members pool money for parties and events, and socialise regularly as a community (Informants 1 and 4). While the culture influences those who spend time on the farm, the farm also influences the community's culture by emphasising the notion that agriculture has a place in urban and suburban contexts. All informants felt pride in the mission and accomplishments of the farm and were gratified to be a part of a positive force in their community. Informants 1 and 3 credited the organipónico with increasing a culture of pride in the community, through its elevation of the community's status.

Hosting Cuban school groups, who learn about and experience nature on the farm, illustrates the farm's focus on education (Informant 4). Young people learn about agriculture/agroecological practices at the farm and get excited about potential careers in agriculture. Food preparation is another part of the traditional culture that the organipónico is striving to preserve and pass on to the younger generations (Informants 2 and 4; farm tour notes). Informant 3 commented on how the farm inspires a strong work ethic in the younger generation of interns, and visiting and full-time workers. Members also value their ability to teach farming skills and traditions to visiting scholars and farmers from within Cuba and from around the world. As opposed to keeping their knowledge proprietary, they have developed a culture of education and the dissemination of knowledge (Informant 2; farm tour notes). This is particularly important for the farm as they are continuously trying new practices to improve their own proficiency in sustainable farming.

Human capital

Skill development, knowledge, and education are at the core of human capital development at the organipónico. When employees come to the farm, they are trained in agroecological practices – some of which are specific to the farm setting, but can also be transferred to their personal lives (Informants 1 and 2). Most employees receive cross-training in a variety of positions as a way to develop them professionally (Informant 5). Farm workers also visit local schools (or school groups visit them) to educate children about agriculture and get them excited about growing food (Informants 1 and 4), thereby transferring knowledge from older adults to younger people and passing on the traditions of sustainable agriculture. In this regard, they have developed an informal mentorship programme (Informant 1). This has helped to reduce the number of young people leaving the community to work elsewhere. The farm also fosters employees' self-esteem and sense of purpose (Informants 1, 3, and 4). This increased self-esteem is also related to bonding and bridging social capital on the farm through the family-like community they create, and the cultural pride that results from being recognised as leaders in their field.

Social capital

Social capital is at the heart of the success of the organipónico because the organisation exists for the local people (Informants 1, 2, 3, 4, and 5). Three themes emerged indicating increasing social capital among the community because of the farm. First, many residents of the surrounding community have become part of 'farm family' joining the cooperative, thereby increasing and bonding social capital. The informants cited a sense of belonging and reciprocity with the farm and developing close relationships on the farm (Informants 1, 3, and 4). There is low turnover because employees enjoy their work, they do not hurry to leave when their workday ends, and they work towards the common goal of creating a quality product in which they can take pride (Informant 4). Second, the ties between employees and the community are strengthened through parties and other social gatherings which the employees are able to host by pooling money. One informant noted, working at the farm is not just a job, but a place where connections can be formed and strengthened (Informant 3). Third, the farm was established in response to a community need – unavailability of fresh food. Members receive produce for free or reduced prices and the remaining food is supplied to community vendors who sell to surrounding communities, local schools, hospitals, and other businesses (farm tour notes).

Political capital

Data showed that employees feel empowered because of their ability to contribute to decision-making on the farm. At monthly meetings, their voices are heard through open forums and they can vote on decisions impacting the farm – any major decision is submitted to the assembly for everyone to vote. They can also share their concerns and suggest change (Informants 1, 3, and 4). Employees have become comfortable expressing and proposing their ideas freely, knowing that they will be discussed and possibly implemented (Informant 3). Employees also have the opportunity to change jobs on the farms (e.g. between cooking, field work, sales positions) or move upward by indicating to the group that they would like to do another job (Informants 1 and 4). Comparatively, this gives employees more authority over their lives and careers because no government permission is needed to change roles or advance, which is dissimilar to other industries.

Older adults and women are particularly empowered through work on the farm (Informant 4). Older adults bring certain skills and knowledge making them valuable workers for the farm and giving them more purpose in life. Likewise, women are given equal opportunity and voice, where the farm has even implemented policies to make sure that workload is balanced between women and men. This is unique within the context of Cuba and other Latin American countries where traditional gender ideology creates unequal power dynamics. A study by the Center for Democracy in the Americas (2013) found that in the twenty-first century Cuba, gender equality still falls short in the workplace, in the home, and in access to power. Overall, the importance placed on treatment of the employees of the farm coupled with the power they are given to influence decisions on the farm translates into increased political capital on the individual levels for the workers.

Financial capital

Financial capital was frequently mentioned first when informants were asked about the impact of the farm on the local community. The organipónico's main contribution to the tenets of financial capital is in job creation and bringing new money into the community. The farm started with only seven cooperative members, but now has almost 200 workers – 42 of whom are women (Informants 1 and 2). Positions on the farm often pay better than other types of work. For example, doctors, engineers, and former government ministers have left jobs to work on the farm (Informant 1). In addition to better pay, the farm provides a sense of economic security where the employees know that they will always enjoy benefits – including a pay cheque and two meals per day – whether the harvest is good or not (Informants 1 and 2).

The farm reflects an emerging form of small business in the Cuban economy that has the ability to retain more money earned from selling its products rather than relinquishing most of it to the state. Some of the recently implemented economic and agricultural policies have made the farm an attractive employer because employees' quality of life is the focus. While the farm sells most of its produce directly to the local residents, they also sell 5–6% to paladares, restaurants, and hotels outside the community, creating a small ripple effect (Informant 1). The farm has attempted to further expand distribution, but lack of infrastructure has limited the organipónico to supplying nearby businesses (Informant 1).

Built capital

Infrastructure development within the farm is one of the ways in which the farm improved the built capital of the community – bee houses, drying racks, irrigation systems, and insect 'laboratories' are all part of the farm's built environment that support agroecological practices. These built components are also points of interest on farm tours. The farm has also acted as a focal point of the community as it hosts educational workshops for residents. The increased presence of both community and tourist activities has necessitated construction of seating, shelters, eating areas, additional bathrooms, and access to lighting and water which also benefit employees. Revenue from tourism helps to expand agricultural infrastructure, such as the seed house, the solar panels, the humus beds, and the production facility (Informants 1 and 4). Planning for future agroecotourism activity includes a seed breeding facility, larger shelters for classroom space, and possible overnight accommodations (Informant 4).

Agroecotourism impacts

Tourism is supporting the organipónico's original purpose to alleviate food insecurity beyond only acting as a tool for economic diversification, but by influencing other community capitals. The capitals most impacted by tourism were the human, social, political, and financial capitals, which interplayed strongly with each other and caused a ripple effect in other capitals. For example, tourism builds on the financial capital of the farm as an additional revenue stream (e.g. tours, souvenir sales, lunch fees, donations, jobs) which allowed the farm to increase its built capital (e.g. agricultural infrastructure). Moreover, education regarding agroecological practices is the cornerstone for the farm wherein they teach visitors and local residents about the natural environment. This increases confidence and self-esteem of workers because of the demand for their expertise and expands their awareness of global culture and current events not easily accessed in Cuba (human capital). Increased pride and sense of community developed around the farm because of the interest demonstrated by tourists, contributing to cultural capital. Cooperative members have a greater voice because of their tourist audiences that allows them to expand the reach of the knowledge transfer of agroecological practices and the 'real narrative' of Cuban life not confounded by media (political capital). Through tourism, the farm has been able to extend and strengthen social networks (social capital). Table 3 summarises key impacts of tourism to the farm relevant to each community capital.

Table 3. Summary of key impacts of tourism to the farm.

	Community capitals						
	N	C	H	S	P	F	B
Increased income to farm to expand agricultural operations: materials, equipment, infrastructure						+	+
Expanding infrastructure for tourists: shelters, tables, walkways, bathrooms						+	+
Agroeco-education offered to community, tourists, interns, students[SP]			+				
Increase the value of the natural resources as part of the attraction for visitors	+						
The farm (bolstered by tourism income) preserves natural areas in an otherwise suburban setting[SP]	+						
Some visitors do not dispose of foot protection in trash cans	−						
Members are proud of what they are doing at the farm		+	+		+		
Members share pride in being able to do this in Cuba		+					
The farm attracts experts from around the world as a model in urban organic farming (which enhances respect and power)		+			+		
The farm represents the community and the people who live in it; a feeling of unity comes from expressing this to tourists		+	+				
Tourism brings new people with new ideas to the farm		+	+				
Building social capital through growing exposure to other networks (including tourist networks and networks with other coops and individuals/organisations in the local community)[SP]			+	+			
Tourism offers a powerful vehicle for telling visitors about 'real' Cubans		+	+	+			
Expansion of product offerings (because of visitors to the farm – now selling lunches, souvenirs)[SP]						+	
New positions on the farm as a result of more revenue[SP]			+			+	
The type of tourist is an educational tourist so presumably the interactions with the community are more respectful (than the sand, sex, sun, sea tourist)[SP]				+			

Notes: +, positive impact; −, negative impact; SP indicates a spillover impact to the community as a result of tourism to the farm; N, natural; C, cultural; H, human; S, social; P, political; F, financial; B, built.

The findings demonstrate that tourism is creating a 'spiralling-up' effect in the community capitals (Emery & Flora, 2006; Gutierrez-Montes, 2005). As an example related to natural capital, farm cooperative members expressed a strong commitment to preserving the natural landscapes of the farm because of increasing recognition of the value of natural resources as part of what makes the farm a unique tourist attraction (Informant 2). The types of tourists currently visiting the farm are interested in learning about agroecological practices as part of their profession or their hobby; scientists from other countries have been sent to learn practices from the farm (Informants 2 and 4).

Tourism is also spiralling up human capital because many tourists are coming to the farm to learn about organic practices so the farm workers have to transfer their knowledge in a 'train the trainer situation' (Informants 3 and 4). Since most tourists are not Cuban, the human capital effect is significantly broader than the immediate community. This not only increases confidence and self-esteem for the trainers because of the demand for their expertise, but also serves to increase their communication skills. Personal communication skills, while important in any community, may have added importance for Cubans where the freedom to openly communicate is not always encouraged. Interacting with foreign visitors serves to increase international awareness, which is an important element of human capital, but is not easy in Cuba because of citizens' limited access to information external to the central government. Tourism to the farm also influences bridging social capital, as the social network of the farm has expanded tremendously through the exposure the farm gains with visitors. The connection with the surrounding community adds to the 'esprit de corp' of the farm's success. Bonding social capital is deepened, in that community members are unified to give visitors a good experience as an important farm goal.

Political capital of farm members increases because of tourism to the farm. Employees are using the opportunity of hosting tourists on the farm to challenge stereotypes and preconceived ideas about the Cuban people; the 'real' Cuban narrative was an important theme during interviews. A sense of empowerment ensued from their ability to talk directly to the tourists, which in their perspective, allows the tourists to see them outside of how the media portrays them. Informants suggested that discussing Cuban culture was just as important as talking about the actual agricultural practices of the farm (Informants 1 and 4). In that regard, they often have visitors with very strong political questions, which they welcome because they can give them a more localised response. The farm workers are in an interesting position to provide their own opinion because they do not work for the state, allowing them more freedom of expression (Informant 4). The idea of this Cuban narrative was interwoven with the pride and cultural capital that tourism is building for the farm. The farm is bringing status and recognition to the community on a global scale, which illustrates spiralling-up of the community's political capital.

Tours of the farm have created positive economic impact through the sale of souvenirs and lunch (Informants 1, 2, 3, and 4). Souvenirs such as jewellery made from sunflower seeds, coffee beans, and other 'farm materials' are sold on the farm by community residents. A discussion of future initiatives included visitors staying in accommodations on the farm (Informants 2 and 4). Tourists who visit during the summer, when most crops are being grown rather than harvested, give the farm the opportunity to supplement its income during the low-selling and tourist season (Informant 4). Additionally, tourism augments financial capital through donations. The farm, which has become the face of the local community, has begun accepting material donations from visitors such as school and work supplies, and farm equipment (Informant 1).

Extending beyond traditional agritourism, the findings of this study demonstrate the complementary nature of agroecotourism with the core tenets of ecotourism. Likewise, the application of the CCF was shown to be an effective way to examine the adherence of agroecotourism to ecotourism principles as illustrated in the following. The tourism activities on the farm were nature-based (natural capital) and focused on learning (human capital) about the environment and natural resources management. The activities were non-consumptive, non-invasive, and ethically managed activities (thereby minimally affecting natural capital) and, further, extended tourists' knowledge on sustainable practices (human capital). Agroecotourism on the farm benefited the local community through the added economic impact, increased pride/ self-esteem, and creating the opportunity to have their 'voice' heard (financial, human, and political capital), was controlled by the local community which is an anomaly within the socialist society, and through tourism, was continuing to gain the means to expand the farm and its impact to the community (political and built capital).

Conclusion

This paper contributes to the CCF tourism planning literature by applying the framework to a new context, expanding on the limited literature on agroecotourism development, and discussing unique possibilities for tourism in a socialist nation. The paper demonstrates the CCF's utility in scaffolding sustainability goals – when all of the capitals are nurtured, a spiralling-up effect occurs in the community through tourism development (Emery & Flora, 2006). This paper also explores the potential of agroecotourism as an appropriate niche market that can support positive impacts to local communities through their focus on education, sustainability, and community development. As Cavaliere (2010) notes, 'agroecotourism, as an example is an area of tourism that demands more in-depth investigation as it links several methods of improving health and livelihoods' (p. 34). In this regard, this paper provides further evidence of the potential linkage between agroecology and sustainable tourism development goals.

   With continued political reform at a national level in Cuba, policy change is beginning to be felt at the individual level as it pertains to small business development and entrepreneurship in tourism. As part of the 2010 economic reforms set in motion by Raul Castro, self-employment is beginning to be legalised which would allow people to enter into the private business sector. With the potential opportunities opening up through tourism, there is a need to consider how tourism may further impact the farm. What if the visitors change? How will the impacts change with different forms of development? Will tourism become more important than agriculture given its economic impact? Finally, will tourism continue to foster the spiralling-up of all the capitals or could negative impacts cause a spiralling-down?

Disclosure statement

No potential conflict of interest was reported by the authors.

References

Altieri, M. A. (1989). Agroecology: A new research and development paradigm for world agriculture. *Agriculture, Ecosystems & Environment, 27*(1), 37–46.

Altieri, M. A. (2002). Agroecology: The science of natural resource management for poor farmers in marginal environments. *Agriculture, Ecosystems & Environment, 93*(1), 1–24.

Alvarez, J. (2004). *Transformations in Cuban agriculture after 1959* (UF E EDIS document FE 481, pp. 1–9). Gainseville: University of Florida Extension.

Arroyo, G. C., Barbieri, C., & Rozier Rich, S. (2013). Defining agritourism: A comparative study of stakeholders' perceptions in Missouri and North Carolina. *Tourism Management, 37*, 39–47.

Babb, F. E. (2011). Che, Chevys, and Hemingway's Daiquiris: Cuban tourism in a time of globalisation. *Bulletin of Latin American Research, 30*(1), 50–63.

Bagdonis, J. M., Hand, E., Larson, G., Sanborn, M., & Bruening, T. H. (2009). *Agro-ecotourism in Costa Rica: A participatory rural appraisal case study*. 2009 AIAEE Proceedings of the 25th Annual Meeting, San Juan, Puerto Rico.

Becker, H. (2011). Tourism in Cuba: Barriers to economic growth and development. In Bildner Center for Western Hemisphere Studies (Eds.), *Political economy of change in Cuba* (pp. 139–153). NY: The City University of New York.

Bernard, H. R., & Ryan, G. W. (2010). *Analyzing qualitative data: Systematic approaches*. Sage.

Boldak, A., Rudenko, D., Pestis, M., Pestis, P., & Rudenko, E. (2009). *Agroecotourism development in the Republic of Belarus*. Zeszyty Naukowe Szkoły Głównej Gospodarstwa Wiejskiego w Warszawie. Problemy Rolnictwa Światowego, 6, 5–9.

Callaghan, E. G., & Colton, J. (2008). Building sustainable & resilient communities: A balancing of community capital. Environment, *Development and Sustainability, 10*(6), 931–942.

Cavaliere, C. (2010, March). *Sustainable agroecotourism ventures for low-carbon societies*. In Meeting of the Recreation Values & Natural Areas Symposium, Otago.

Center for Democracy of the Americas. (2013). *Women's work: Gender equality in Cuba and the role of women building Cuba's future*. Retrieved December 15, 2015, from http://democracyinamericas.org/pdfs/CDA_Womens_Work.pdf

Choo, H., & Jamal, T. (2009). Tourism on organic farms in South Korea: A new form of ecotourism. *Journal of Sustainable Tourism, 17*(4), 431–454.

Copeland, C., Jolly, C., & Thompson, H. (2011). The history and potential of trade between Cuba and the U.S. *Journal of Economics and Business, 2*(3), 163–174.

Dalgaard, T., Hutchings, N. J., & Porter, J. R. (2003). Agroecology, scaling and interdisciplinarity. *Agriculture, Ecosystems & Environment, 100*(1), 39–51.

Davis, J. H. (2015). U.S. eases some limits on Cuban travel and commerce. *The New York Times*. Retrieved December 15, 2015, from http://www.nytimes.com/2015/09/19/world/americas/us-cuba-relations.html

Embassy of Canada to Cuba. (2013). *Canada – Cuba relations*. Government of Canada. Retrieved December 16, 2015, from http://www.canadainternational.gc.ca/cuba/bilateral_relations_bilaterales/canada_cuba.aspx?lang=eng

Emery, M. F., & Flora, C. (2006). Spiraling-up: Mapping community transformation with community capitals framework. *Community Development, 37*(1), 19–35.

Fennell, D. A. (2008). *Ecotourism: An introduction* (3rd ed.). London: Routledge.

Flint, R. W. (2010). Seeking resiliency in the development of sustainable communities. *Research in Human Ecology, 17*(1), 44–57.

Flora, C. B., & Flora, J. L. (1993, September). Entrepreneurial social infrastructure: A necessary ingredient. *The ANNALS of the American Academy of Political and Social Science, 529*, 48–58. Retrieved from http://www.ag.iastate.edu/centers/rdev/pubs/flora/title.htm

Flora, C. B., Flora, J. L., & Gasteyer, S. (2015). *Rural communities: Legacy + Change*. Boulder, CO: Westview Press.

Flora, C. B., Emery, M., Fey, S., & Bregendahl, C. (2005, December 12–13). *Community capitals: A tool for evaluating strategic interventions and projects*. 2005 Working session on community capitals framework: Research, evaluation, practice. Retrieved December 30, 2006, from http://www.ag.iastate.edu/centers/rdev/newsletter/june97/build-soc-capital.html

Flora, C. B., & Gillespie, A. H. (2009). Making healthy choices to reduce childhood obesity: Community capitals and food and fitness. *Community Development, 40*(2), 114–122.

Gao, J., Barbieri, C., & Valdivia, C. (2014). Agricultural landscape preferences: Implications for agritourism development. *Journal of Travel Research, 53*(3), 366–379. doi:10.1177/0047287513496471

Gliessman, S. (2012). Agroecology and interculturality. *Journal of Sustainable Agriculture, 36* (2), 151–152.

Gliessman, S. (2015). *Agroecology: The ecology of sustainable food systems* (2nd ed.). Santa Cruz, CA: CRC Press.

Goldstein, T. (1995). Interviewing in a multicultural/multilingual setting. *TESOL Quarterly, 29*(3), 587–593. doi:10.2307/3588078

Griffin, T. (2013). Visiting friends and relatives tourism and implications for community capital. *Journal of Policy Research in Tourism, Leisure and Events, 5*(3), 233–251.

Gutierrez-Montes, I. (2005). *Healthy communities equals healthy ecosystems? Evolution (and breakdown) of a participatory ecological research project towards a community Natural Resource Management Process, San Miguel Chimalapa (Mexico)* (PhD dissertation). Iowa State University, Ames, IA.

Gutierrez-Montes, I., Emery, M., & Fernandez-Baca, E. (2009). The sustainable livelihoods approach and the community capitals framework: The importance of system-level approaches to community change efforts. *Community Development, 40*(2), 106–113.

Holmgren, D. (2011). *Permaculture: Principles & pathways beyond sustainability*. Hepburn Springs, VIC.: Holmgren Design Services.

Kline, C., & Oliver, J. (2015). Beyond economic benefits: Exploring the effects of festivals and events on community capitals [book chapter]. In T. Pernecky, & O. Moufakkir (Eds.), *Ideological, social and cultural aspects of events* (pp. 171–181). Boston, MA: CABI.

Kuo, N. W., Chen, Y. J., & Huang, C. L. (2006). Linkages between organic agriculture and agro-ecotourism. *Renewable Agriculture and Food Systems, 21*(4), 238–244.

Lima, I. B., & d'Hauteserre, A. (2011). Community capitals and ecotourism for sustainable livelihoods. *Anatolia – An International Journal of Tourism and Hospitality Research, 22*(2), 184–203.

McGehee, N. G., Lee, S., O'Bannon, T. L., & Perdue, R. R. (2010). Tourism-related social capital and its relationship with other forms of capital: An exploratory study. *Journal of Travel Research, 49*(4), 486–500.

Myrdal, G. (1957). *Economic theory and underdeveloped regions*. London: Gerald Duckworth.

Nelson, E., Scott, S., Cukier, J., & Galán, Á. L. (2009). Institutionalizing agroecology: Successes and challenges in Cuba. *Agriculture and Human Values, 26*(3), 233–243.

Patton, M. Q. (1987). *How to use qualitative methods in evaluation*. London: Sage.

Pender, J., Marré, A., & Reeder, R. (2012, March). *Rural wealth creation: Concepts, strategies and measures* (Economic Research Report No. ERR-131). Retrieved from the U.S. Department of Agriculture, Economic Research Service website, http://www.ers.usda.gov/publications/err-economic-research-report/err131.aspx

Pérez, L. A. (2011). *Cuba: Between reform and revolution*. New York: Oxford University Press.

Peters, P. (2012). *Cuba's entrepreneurs: Foundation of a new private sector*. Retrieved from the Lexington Institute website, http://www.lexingtoninstitute.org/library/resources/documents/Cuba/ResearchProducts/CubaEntrepreneurs.pdf

Pierce, J., & McKay, J. (2008). On community capitals as we see them through photovoice: Cowell oyster industry in South Australia. *Australasian Journal of Environmental Management, 15*(3), 159–168.

Privitera, D. (2009, December). *Factors of development of competitiveness: The case of organic-agritourism.* EAAE seminar 'the role of knowledge, innovation and human capital in multifunctional agriculture and territorial Rural development', Belgrade, Republic of Serbia, pp. 9–11.

Pujol, J. (2011, August). *Main problems faced by the Cuban economy and what the government is doing to try to solve them.* Cuba in transition: Papers and proceedings of the twenty-first annual meeting of the association for the study of the cuban economy, Miami, FL.

Saldana, J. (2009). *The coding manual for qualitative researchers.* Thousand Oaks, CA: Sage.

Sharpley, R., & Knight, M. (2009). Tourism and the state in Cuba: From the past to the future. *International Journal of Tourism Research, 11*(3), 241–254.

Sseguya, H., Mazur, R. E., & Masinde, D. (2009). Harnessing community capitals for livelihood enhancement: Experiences from a livelihood program in rural Uganda. *Community Development, 40*(2), 123–138.

Wezel, A., Bellon, S., Doré, T., Francis, C., Vallod, D., & David, C. (2009). Agroecology as a science, a movement and a practice. A review. *Agronomy for Sustainable Development, 29*, 503–515.

World Travel & Tourism Council. (2015). *Travel & Tourism Economic Impact 2015.* Cuba.

Zahra, A., & McGehee, N. G. (2013). Volunteer tourism: A host community capital perspective. *Annals of Tourism Research, 42*, 22–45.

Ecotourism influence on community needs and the functions of protected areas: a systems thinking approach

Moren Tibabo Stone and Gyan P. Nyaupane

ABSTRACT

Using the community capitals framework with a systems thinking lens, we explored how the development of ecotourism has influenced changes in community needs that in turn have influenced the functions of protected areas (PAs). Data collected through semi-structured interviews and secondary sources, the Chobe Enclave Conservation Trust, located adjacent to Chobe National Park in Botswana, provide the research context. Results indicated that ecotourism development has led to stock accumulation of the natural capital in the form of wildlife. On the other hand, ecotourism development through the prevalence of cash flow and reinvestment in agriculture transformed agricultural practices and increased the demand of land for ploughing and henceforth heightened community–wildlife conflicts. Consequently, competing use of land for agriculture, wildlife, and tourism establishments has the potential to alter the functions of PAs in their effort to accommodate new changes. The domino effect induced by the introduction of ecotourism in a rural and isolated area leads to community prosperity that changes community needs and priorities, triggering unintended environmental consequences that further require PAs adaptive mitigation interventions.

Introduction

In the developing world, nature-based tourism resources are primarily hosted by protected areas (PAs) in the form of wildlife and wilderness (Ghimire & Pimbert, 1997). In the beginning of their demarcation and development, PAs were particularly known for their extensive resource separation and the economic hardships that they posed to rural communities (Sanderson, 2005). However, the realisation that PAs have the potential to host tourism and improve communities' livelihoods in the early 1990s (IUCN, 1994; Naughton-Treves, Holland, & Brandon, 2005) led to a reversal of roles. Now they aim to play both conservation and development roles.

Biodiversity conservation and development 'paradigm wars' fought in the 1970s and 1980s have somewhat calmed down, and ecotourism development has gained some acceptance in the use of PAs as spaces that host biodiversity resources. As PAs serve different stakeholders, they have been exposed to many transformations and subjected to growing marketisation, multiple competing uses, changing rural economies, and technological modernisation (Nyaupane & Poudel, 2011). Many of these changes may be directly linked to tourism development as a new comer in PAs' resources use (Stone & Nyaupane, 2016). In PAs and tourism discourse, this issue has received secondary attention while the primary focus is still on rural social security and the conservation of PAs (Gossling, Hall, & Weaver, 2009).

There has been a global call to link the conservation of PAs and community development through tourism development (IUCN, 1994). This linkage has been promoted through integrated conservation and development projects to engender support for conservation among communities living in and adjacent to PAs (Heinen, 1993; Sekhar, 2003). For communities living within or around PAs, tourism's role is multifaceted, including financial (Saayman & Saayman, 2006), non-financial livelihood, empowerment, and environmental services (Ashley & Elliot, 2003). Literature generally supports the view that communities will only support conservation if the benefits of living with natural resources outweigh costs (Mbaiwa, 2011; Mbaiwa & Stronza, 2011). Several studies have concluded that costs associated with conservation, such as wildlife depredation of crops and livestock, have negative effects on local community attitudes, while benefits may have positive effects (Fiallo & Jacabson, 1995; Heinen, 1993; Walpole & Goodwin, 2001). In view of these opposing viewpoints, it is important to assess how benefits from tourism may have an impact on changes in community needs using the community capitals framework (CCF) underpinnings as a system thinking approach.

Systems thinking approach

A system is defined as 'a set of connected things, an organised or interrelated group of things; orderliness' (Anon, 1991, p. 1085). The system thinking approach seeks to understand system behaviour by examining 'the whole' instead of its parts (Forrester, 1961). This approach draws on engineering control theory and the modern theory of nonlinear dynamical systems (Sterman, 2002). That is, we should conceptualise PAs, ecotourism, and livelihoods as a complex system, consisting of multiple interacting components. Henceforth, this paper's argument is premised on the background that ecotourism, PAs, and community livelihoods operate as a complex system, and the relationship contains myriad factors and activities that are inter-dependent (i.e. economic, social, environmental, cultural, political, human, and policy factors) (Walker, Greiner, McDonald, & Lyne, 1998).

Appraising tourism literature on systems thinking, indications are that tourism studies first applied these ideologies during the 1970s (Holling & Chambers, 1973; Moser & Petersen, 1981). Over time, particularly the last 25 years, a significant number of scholarly contributions on sustainable tourism development have been made (e.g. Butler, 1999; Gossling, Hall, Ekstrom, Engeset, & Aall, 2012; Hunter, 1997; Mbaiwa, 2011; Mbaiwa & Stronza, 2011; Stone & Stone, 2011; Swarbrooke, 1999). These seminal works offer useful insight mainly in the areas of tourism participation and empowerment, stakeholder collaboration, and resource management techniques that have helped to advance and operationalise the concept of systems thinking. Nevertheless, it is argued here that future progress will be severely hampered if more attention is not paid to progress in sustainable tourism development informed by a systems thinking approach. Lenao (2013) suggests this is due to a lack of integrated and sustainable tourism development due to poor planning and implementation of tourism-related projects. Comprehensive sustainable tourism needs to go beyond focusing on the economic, social, and environmental benefits to include cultural, human, and political planning (Saarinen & Lenao, 2014). Gossling et al. (2009) are sceptical that moving to more sustainable tourism is a very difficult task as it requires transformations of well-established and interlocking systems and social practices. Credit of, and requirement to these commitments is now needed within tourism operations. This is conjecture, however, because of prevalent structural deficiencies, there is a dearth of literature on this topic (Gossling et al., 2012; Hall, 2011; Sharpley, 2009; Strickland-Munro, Allison, & Moore, 2010). Tourism is often managed with inadequate knowledge, particularly of the approach in which the entire tourism system functions, and of the science that drives it. Thus, the literature presents that sustainable tourism as a paradox. At one level, sustainable tourism is a success given the concept's diffusion among industry, government, academics, and policy actors, yet, it is simultaneously a policy failure given the continued growth in the environmental impacts of tourism in absolute terms. Bramwell and Lane (2013) suggest that progress towards sustainable tourism is at best almost static, and believe that we are moving backwards. Sharpley (2009) considers sustainable tourism as deficient paradigm and calls for alternative approaches. Nevertheless, sustainability depends not just on those key elements often referred to as the 'tourism industry' but on the whole 'comprehensive tourism system' (Farrell & Twining-Ward, 2004). Henceforth, systems thinking approach in tourism studies is critical to understanding how tourism is organised.

PA's acceptance of the tourism industry requires adaptation to new situations and challenges that come with this conservation and development evolution nexus. Hence, there has been extended debate about how to conceptualise PAs, tourism, and community livelihoods (Gossling et al., 2012; Hall, 2011; Nyaupane & Poudel, 2011; Strickland-Munro et al., 2010), giving rise to a number of models that attempt to represent the relationship. A number of such conceptualisations of understanding under the banner of 'conservation and development nexus' attempt to provide guidance about 'managing' physical and social relationships among conservation and development in response to growing environmental and development complexity. For instance, Budowski (1976) developed a model that explains three types of relationships (i.e. conflict, coexistence, and symbiosis); Carter (1994) conceptualised four possible links: win/win, win/lose, lose/win, and lose/lose, and Salafsky and Wollenberg (2000) proposed three scenarios: no linkage, indirect linkage, and direct linkage. The theoretical argument is that the conservation and development nexus debate cannot objectively be understood in all cases using simple uni-directional 'cause and effect' models, particularly if they do not take into consideration the complexity aspects of interaction. We argue that there must be an appraisal of complexity among ecotourism, PAs, and community livelihoods with a framework approach that gives a more robust appreciation of complex connections. Conceptualising this complex relationship in a systems thinking approach has the propensity to capture the essence of tacit knowledge that can inform intervention management measures.

In the context of this paper, the CCF is used to understand the stock (i.e. identifying assets in each capital) and flow (i.e. the types of capital invested) among community capitals as a result of the interaction between PAs, ecotourism, and community livelihoods, and how the impacts of these stock and flow affect the system. We use a case study approach, where the Chobe Enclave Conservation Trust (CECT), a community-based organisation (CBO) participating in an eco-tourism project, adjacent to Chobe National Park (CNP), Botswana, provides the context of the study.

Community capital framework

Developed by Flora (2005), the CCF provides a tool for analysing how communities work. The CCF consists of seven types of capitals – natural, cultural, human, social, political, financial, and built (Emery, Fey, & Flora, 2006) – as illustrated in Figure 1. The framework offers an approach to assess community and development efforts from a systems thinking perspective, by identifying assets in each capital (stock), the types of capital invested (flow), the interaction among the types of capital, and the consequential impacts on them (Emery et al., 2006).

Communities are systems that have inflows and outflows, ups and downs, progression and regression (Jacobs, 2007). Capital assets can be wisely invested, combined, and/or exchanged to create more community resources. They can also be squandered or accumulated if not used wisely (Emery et al., 2006). If the assets are sustainably used, the outcomes are healthy ecosystems, vibrant regional economies, social equity, and empowerment (Flora, Flora, & Fey,

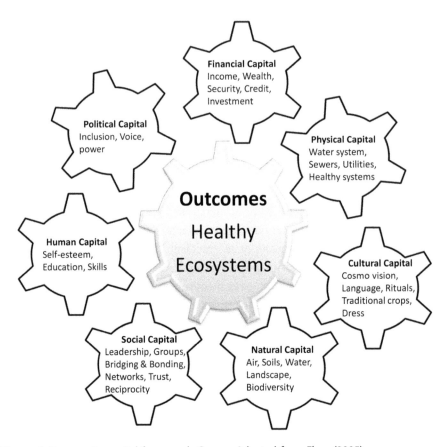

Figure 1. Community capital framework. Source: Adapted from Flora (2005).

2004). An overview of the seven types of community capitals is summarised in Table 1.

While the types of capital have been separated into seven discrete categories, each has a connection to other types of capital types. In order to survive and prosper in what can often be difficult circumstances, communities pursue a 'livelihood strategy', comprised of a number of different activities such as farming, off-farm employment, fishing, hunting, and gathering (De Sherbinin et al., 2008). In order to engage in these activities, communities mobilise the types of capital at their disposal. An array of livelihood approaches emphasises capabilities of communities, based on the recognition that even the poorest communities hold wealth in at least some of their capitals (De Sherbinin et al., 2008). It is the combination of these assets that defines the socio-economics of a community depending on its capability (Sen, 2009) to harness available capitals. For example, a community that liquidates forest resources in order to finance education is substituting natural capital for human capital, which may in turn yield employment opportunities that yield a steady stream of financial capital, which may then be depleted in order to invest in physical assets such as cattle, houses, and/or vehicles. The CCF

Table 1. Summary of community capitals.

Capitals	Descriptions
Social	This is the networking account. It includes the close bonds between and among family and friends, communities, groups, organisations, networks and trust in the community, the sense of belonging, and bonds between people. It can influence, as well as be influenced by, the stock and flows of other capitals
Human	This is the human resource 'people' account. It includes leadership capabilities, knowledge, wisdom, information, and skills possessed by the people who live in the community
Natural	This is the environmental account. It includes the resources that exist in the natural world. Some of which may include but are not limited to; the soil, lakes, natural resources, nature's beauty, rivers, forests, wildlife and local landscape. Communities work with these resources to meet livelihoods needs
Financial	This is the financial account. It includes the resources related to money and access to funding, wealth, charitable giving, grants
Physical/ built	This is the building and infrastructure account. It includes the following; houses, schools, businesses, clinics, libraries, water systems, electrical grid, communication systems, roads, transportation systems
Cultural	This is the account for community cultural resources. The way communities view the world. Culture defines the traditional ways of doing and being – habits and attitudes. It includes dances, stories, heritage, food, and traditions and also values and connections to the spirit. Cultural capital is also a resource to attract tourism
Political	This account represents power and community connections to people who have power. Communities draw upon this resource when they unite to solve a controversial issue. Political capital is built by making connections with political and community leaders both inside and outside the community. It also refers to the ability of people to find their own voice and to engage in actions that contribute to the well-being of their community

Sources: Aigner, Flora, and Hernandez (2001); Emery et al. (2006); Flora et al. (2004, 2006).

offers an alternative approach to assessing community and development efforts from a systems perspective by identifying assets in each capital (stock), the types of capital invested (flow), the interaction among the capitals, and the consequential impacts across types of capital (Emery et al., 2006). In tourism contexts, some researchers believe certain community capitals as being more deterministic of success in community tourism projects. For instance, Bebbington (1999) and Jones (2005) prefer social capital built on the view that trust and reciprocity lubricate cooperation through reduced transaction costs. Others (e.g. Boggs, 2001; Portes, 2000) argue that the focus on only one form of capital might be detrimental to the community's overall well-being.

In evaluating literature on the effectiveness of using CCF, Fey, Bregendahl, and Flora (2006) preferred CCF over the Sustainable Livelihood Framework (SLF) as the SLF has only five capitals as opposed to the CCF's seven. Fey et al. (2006) reported that choosing indicators and measuring community capitals were challenging as some capitals overlap. When studying community empowerment, Laverack and Wallerstein (2001) found that the difficulty with measurement does not lie in finding forms of capital within a community, but rather in finding a way to measure how capital is invested to affect a community's capacity. Despite limitations of the CCF's performance, Saggers (2003) found that it was an effective framework for assessing community service and development. Serageldin and Steer (1994) suggest that sustainability scholars should think of sustainable development in terms of patterns in the accumulation of, and substitution among different types of community capitals.

Sustainability, therefore, requires a balance between being economically viable, preserving the resilience of cultural integrity and social cohesion, and maintaining the status quo of the physical environment (Altman & Finlayson, 1993).

In linking the CCF and community needs, researchers show that changes in community needs can be evolutionary in nature or externally facilitated wherein groups of people or government programmes are established to modify segments of community life (Holmberg & Dobyns, 1962; Lippett, Jeannie, & Bruce, 1958). Community changes can also be unintentionally facilitated by socio-cultural drift. For instance, engineers build roads or mine owners introduce mining activities inadvertently changing community life (Sanders, 1958). Communities exposed to new socio-economic situations may over time be influenced by new economic patterns, and in turn community value systems may shift (Sanders, 1958). The emerging economic patterns or drifts are explained by community capitals (Alkire, 2002).

When one type of capital is emphasised over alternatives, other assets are decapitalised, and the economy, environment, or social equity can thus be compromised (Deneulin, 2008). To understand how community capitals get transformed, first it is crucial to understand the influence of the world economy. In the past, small size and isolation combined to produce relatively homogeneous rural cultures, economies based on natural resources, and a strong sense of local identity (Flora & Emery, 2006). However, globalisation, connectivity, and accompanying shifting income distributions altered the character of rural communities (Sen, 2009). Today, not only are rural and urban areas alike being drawn into a world economy, but the character of the economy is changing (Flora et al., 2004). With these situations, many communities feel the impacts of numerous features of dominant metropolitan areas that have an effect on the organisation of their capitals (Sanders, 1958).

The argument is that social and economic organisational changes wrought by macro processes and powerful forces of urbanisation, industrialisation, bureaucratisation, and centralisation influence rural autonomous communities in their decision-making and absorb them into a mass society, changing community needs and aligning them with those of powerful forces (Summers, 1986). These forces are accelerated by the process of globalisation, and there are slim chances for communities to resist these forces since they propel interdependence, destroy autonomy of societies, and render small rural communities powerless (Moxley, 1985). It follows from this discussion that if we want to understand the relationship between PAs, tourism, and community livelihoods, we must first specify its parts in terms of its capitals. It is the transition from one level of upward community mobility to another that leads to changes in community needs (Ghimire, & Pimbert, 1997). In the context of this paper, the CCF is used to understand the flow among the capitals as a result of the interaction between the PA, tourism, and community livelihoods.

Methods

Study area

The study was carried out in the CECT, located adjacent to CNP in Botswana. The research was conducted in CH1&2, which are concession areas belonging to CECT (Figure 2). The study area (i.e. CECT) was chosen because it is the first community project in Botswana to be engaged in community-based ecotourism, and this provided the foundation for ecotourism projects in Botswana and other African countries. The CECT comprises the five villages of Mabele, Kavimba, Kachikau, Satau, and Parakarungu in northern Botswana. The villages are located on a belt that runs along the Chobe Basin forming an enclave, hence the name. The villages are located in a buffer zone that is divided into two controlled hunting areas (CHAs): CH1 used for hunting tourism and CH2 is used for photographic tourism. In terms of its bioeconomics, CECT is situated within the second most important wildlife and tourism area in Botswana after the Okavango Delta (Jones, 2003). CECT is run by a board of trustees from the five member villages. Due to participation in an ecotourism project, the five villages grouped together to become one beneficiary 'community' called the CECT for convenient ecotourism participation and administration purposes. Therefore, CECT is a CBO representing CECT villages through the creation of a board of trustees. Two individuals are elected from each village to sit on the board, and chiefs by virtue of their positions are *ex-officio* members. In total, the CECT board is made up of 15 members, and is elected for a three-year term.

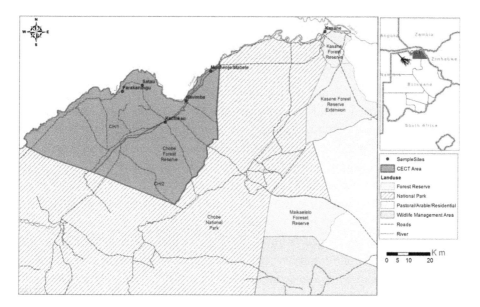

Figure 2. (Colour online) Study area.

Residents of the five villages are mainly the *Basubiya* tribe; hence there is not much difference among the villages in terms of socio-economics. The CECT community has a mixed economy based on three main domains: subsistence livestock rearing, crop production, and wage employment. With more than 650 mm per annum, the Enclave receives the highest rainfall in Botswana and is within the area most suitable for rain-fed cropping (Jones, 2002). Crop production is undertaken by 86% of the households and livestock is owned by 75% of households (Jones, 2003). The CNP occupies more than 10,000 km^2 of land while the CECT occupies about 1690 km^2 (Jones, 2003). The estimated population of the Enclave community is 4500 (Botswana, 2011).

The 'community' refers to the five villages represented by CECT, and more emphasis has been placed on geographical definition sense. We do not assume that CECT community is a coherent entity, but because the data were collected from the five villages, they are referred to as the CECT community.

Data collection

Primary and secondary data were collected. Primary data sources included individual semi-structured interviews with key government officers, and household heads or individuals 18 years and older, when household heads were not present. The interview method was chosen in order to ensure respondents understood the questions asked and to acquire rich ethnographic data, which helps to understand the changing relationships among various community capitals. Interviews took place between the months of May and August 2013. This was an opportune time period since it was the dry season and most participants were in their homes rather than out ploughing fields. A household list from CECT was used to randomly pick household interviewees. Forty-seven interviews were conducted with the number of participants guided by the attainment of theoretical saturation (Patton, 1990).

Six of the 47 participants were government officials from the Departments of Police, Land Board, Wildlife, Tourism, Crop Production, and Animal Production. They were selected to represent government offices actively involved in tourism, conservation, and livelihood improvement. Hence, information on why and how the project was set up, the daily operations of the enterprise, the level of interaction and community participation, benefits and losses derived, and its performance were collected. Twenty-seven of the participants were female and 20 were male (see Table 2)

Participants' ages ranged from 19 to 72, and their education ranged from never-been-to-school to tertiary education. All household heads' interviews were conducted in *Setswana* while government officers' interviews were conducted in English. The duration of the interviews ranged from 40 to 80 minutes. With the exception of three individuals, all interviews were audio

Table 2. Respondents' composition.

Village name	Gender		Total
	Male	Female	
Mabele	5	3	8
Kavimba	4	5	9
Kachikau	3	6	9
Satau	4	5	9
Parakarungu	1	6	7
Government officials	3	2	5
Total	20	27	47

recorded. For the three, shorthand entries were performed as they did not feel comfortable with their voices being recorded.

An interview technique referred to as funnelling was adopted (Patton, 1990), whereby the interview process started with broad questions on the community's perceptions on PAs, livelihoods, and changes in community needs, followed by more specific inquiries about particular positions. Some general interview questions included: 'What does the CNP as a PA represent to you', 'Describe any relationship you may have with the CNP', and 'What are changes in your lifestyle that have been facilitated by your participation in ecotourism?' To safeguard trustworthiness of data, procedures were undertaken to seek clarification and explanations during and immediately after the interview, as recommended by Harrison, MacGibbon, and Morton (2001). Secondary data sources used included CECT and government reports, which were useful in complementing the primary data. Examples of secondary sources included CECT land use management plan, constitution, consultancy technical and financial reports, board and annual general meetings minutes. Governments' reports included mainly policies, strategic plans, CECT crop production and human wildlife conflicts records, and published and unpublished data.

Data analysis

The analytical procedure was based on techniques proposed by extant interpretive studies (Miles & Huberman, 1994). The first step entailed transcribing the data and translating it from *Setswana* to English. One of the authors is fluent in both languages, which made the interview and translation process easier.

Second, a modified grounded theory analysis approach (Padgett, 2008) was employed to analyse data. The analytic procedure predominantly entailed a holistic content perspective whereby the researchers explored the central meaning of participant narratives (Lieblich, Tuval-Mashiach, & Zilber, 1998). As suggested by Denzin and Lincoln (2000), transcripts were first read several times to get a sense of the data. The conceptual framework was used to define broad categories (seven capitals); sub categories were developed through open coding as they emerged from the data (under each capital category). A defined codebook with detailed descriptions of each code category was developed after four transcripts had been coded to help consistently and systematically code all transcripts. Chunks of text were assigned labels during the first reading of transcripts. The development of codes was guided by content analysis based on the inductive approach (Miles & Huberman, 1994), and involved the identification of words, phrases, sentences, or paragraphs that conveyed a particular message relating to the community's perceptions. For example, open coding yielded a list of texts that mentioned benefits and constraints brought by ecotourism such as money, tractors, lodges, human–wildlife conflicts, and changes in community needs in several contexts. After open coding was performed, focused coding was then applied to winnow down the codes (Charmaz, 2006), facilitated by the memo technique, a widely used method for recording relations among themes (Bernard & Ryan, 2003). For example, under each category (capital), its contributions in terms of facilitating or lack of, in community participation in ecotourism were identified. This process of analysis focused more on manifest rather than latent content texts.

Finally, group-like codes were treated as common themes. For example, abundant wildlife resources were linked with human–wildlife conflicts; cultural resistance was linked with slow adoption of ecotourism; more ploughing hectares were linked with availability of tractors, etc.

Findings

Changes in community capitals

Based on the household and key informant interviews and secondary data sources, the development of wildlife-based ecotourism in the community can be traced back to 1989 when a series of meetings between the community and the government through the Department of Wildlife and National Parks (DWNP) were held to discuss issues of human–wildlife conflicts and potential mitigations. Apart from DWNP, other key players included NGOs such as Kalahari Conservation Society (KCS), Chobe Wildlife Trust, and the donor – the United States Agency for International Development (USAID) (Jones, 2003; Nchunga, 2003).

The role of NGOs was vital in building the community trust, bonding, and cohesiveness – social capitals that in turn created the foundation for adopting ecotourism. Capacity building training and workshops through the financial assistance of USAID contributed to the building of financial and human capital deficits. Table 3 summarises changes that occurred in community capitals before and after the adoption of ecotourism as a form of livelihood.

The natural capital was abundant in the form of wildlife, but due to lack of organisation of other forms of capital, the natural capital was viewed by the community as a nuisance as it was destroying the community's property. An interview with a representative of the Department of Tourism (DoT) revealed that NGOs had to work with the community to break down beliefs embedded in

Table 3. Changes in community capitals after ecotourism.

Types of capitals	Status of community capitals	
	Before ecotourism adoption	After ecotourism adoption
Social capital	Lack of village organisation, no network and partnership with safari companies, government, NGOs, donors, lack of trust among five villages and other stakeholders	CECT formation, networks, and partnerships with private companies – hunting and photography, safari companies, donors and NGOs, government. Departments, hand craft and dancing groups, joint venture agreements and partnerships to run CHAs, strengthened social cohesion, better relationships with conservation officials
Political capital	Lack of: community voice, tourism institution, leadership skills in tourism, devolution of power to manage wildlife	Formation of board to run CECT, CECT constitution, CECT land use and management plans, CHAs development, community decision-making in ecotourism income distribution. Community consultations – annual general meetings
Financial capital	Lack of funds to venture into ecotourism	Financial assistance through donor agencies – ADF, AWF, KCS, USAID. Revenue generated from wild animals quota, lodge, campsites, employment, tractors, staged community dances and handcraft wares
Human capital	Lack of capacity and human skills to apply for funds and run ecotourism business	Training workshops for skills & capacity building by government, donors and NGOs agencies (e.g. USAID, AWF), NGOs (KCS). Hiring of trained and competent professionals – CECT manager, programme officer, and accountant
Physical capital	Lack of ecotourism infrastructure: campsites, lodges, vehicles	CECT offices, lodge, campsites, six tractors procured with ploughing equipment, corn grinding mill, shops, 6 tents and their accessories. Changes in house structures. Fencing ploughing fields
Natural capital	Abundance of natural resources in the form of wildlife and wilderness	Photography and hunting tourism, legal harvesting of wild resources, emergence of wildlife-management areas, appreciation of wildlife resources, commoditisation of wildlife resources, heightened human–wildlife conflicts, blocking of wildlife corridors through fencing, wildlife hurting and killings through crops fence entanglements
Cultural capital	Cultural resistance to adopt ecotourism	Funding through CECT: cultural dance and handcrafts groups, cultural self-confidence gained and cultural identity. Commoditisation of culture and high consumption of handcraft raw material

their cultural capital that viewed wild animals as a nuisance. They had to shift their views towards a greater understanding that bringing wildlife-based eco-tourism as a possible venture can actually turn natural capital, mainly wildlife, into a useful resource. An interview with the DWNP officer indicated that due to the history and relations the community had with issues of wildlife, the community believed it had no voice, power, and/or connections to people who had power (political capital) to adopt ecotourism as a form of livelihood because the community believed wildlife belonged to the government. NGOs took almost five years working with the community to organise its capital before the adoption of ecotourism. This was highlighted by a DWNP official who commented:

> We had to organize ourselves first since 1989 to 1993, due to lack of resources we had
> to ask for assistance from the government, donors and NGOs to compensate for the
> resources the community did not have, but it was difficult to get the project
> running, hence it took long time to bring such stakeholders on board.

In 1993, the five villages elected a committee to form the CECT board. External assistance was crucial in organising the community social capital as the foundation for community participation in ecotourism. Informal discussions with the Departments of Animal and Crop Productions indicated that due to high wildlife numbers, especially the so-called problem animals – elephants, buffalos, zebras, wild dogs, lions, hyenas, and baboons – in the CNP, human–wildlife conflicts were endemic as these species wandered beyond the park's boundaries and destroyed community crops and livestock. To manage the high wildlife numbers, informal interviews with DWNP indicated that with the help of the Department of Tourism and Wildlife, consumptive wildlife-based ecotourism in the form of wildlife hunting quotas was introduced in 1993. The wildlife quota is determined by the population of the supposed 'problem animals'. A buffer zone was created between CNP and the community to provide wildlife-controlled hunting areas (CHAs) where the community is engaged in wildlife-management practices. CH1 and CH2 (see Figure 2) are subleased to private safari companies for hunting and photographic tourism, respectively. Wildlife from the CNP spills over and recharges wildlife numbers in CH1 and CH2 and enhances the quality of wildlife targeted for hunting and photographic purposes, thus safari companies find it highly appealing to engage in business with the CECT community.

Before the CECT's formation in 1993, the community was not organised to engage in wildlife ecotourism projects; hence, the community social and political capital was not structured and strategically placed to benefit from the abundant natural capital. During household interviews, a resident from Mabele, age 61, expressed the political deficit as a detriment to participation in ecotourism:

> We were good only with agriculture production but we failed to have seasoned leaders
> to lead us in ecotourism ventures as tourism was foreign and difficult to conceptualize
> as a livelihoods option even though we had a lot of wildlife resources; to us wildlife was
> synonymous with crop destruction.

The formation of CECT was motivated by the availability of abundant natural capital in the form of wildlife. The government departments and NGOs provided technical and coaching assistance on management issues; for example, informal discussions with key government informants; DWNP provided technical assistance on conservation issues, in line with national policies, while the DoT helped with sustainable tourism product development; and Botswana Tourism Organization (BTO) provided assistance on marketing strategies. This process has enhanced the community's social and political capital through collaboration, networking, and partnerships between and among stakeholders as observed by a male BTO officer:

Tourism is a sensitive business that needs an array of skills and resources; from political to cultural will, human to financial resources, natural to physical infrastructure that communities may fail to satisfy on their own, hence our involvement as experts to help communities.

In realising difficulties in managing natural resources, CECT developed a constitution that guides the board on day-to-day management of tourism activities. The constitution improved the community's decision-making process, nurturing the community's political capital and empowering the community as a document of reference in running CECT business. To further build and strengthen the management of CHAs, through financial assistance from USAID and the African Wildlife Foundation (AWF), CECT developed a Land Use and Management Plan for the buffer zone. These developments enhanced CECT's political capital, enabling CECT to execute informed decisions through the guidance of the constitution. This has created an open dialogue between CECT and the government and promoted the devolution of authority over wildlife back to the villages. A CECT male board member, Parakarungu, age 52, remarked:

> Before the development of the CECT constitution and land use management plan, it was difficult for the CECT board to have a common understanding when taking decisions that concerns the project, and the existence of the land use plan is instrumental in preventing free-open-access-use of wildlife resources [in CH1 and CH2].

Through participation in ecotourism, the community has created substantial revenue generation. Income generation occurs at both community and household levels. At the community level, income is derived from the wildlife hunting quota, photography, Ngoma lodge, camping sites, tractors, grinding mill, brick moulding, telephone shops, and general dealer stores and also represent the accumulation of community physical assets. The revenue generated has boosted the community's financial capital. At the household level, community members earn income/wages from employment within CECT and in local tourism establishments. The CECT Annual General meeting minutes (2011) indicate that a total of 105 people are employed in tourism and related establishments, and 36 community members are employed by CECT as tractor drivers, shop assistants, telephone shop operators, brick moulders, camp site workers, and grinding mill attendants. During the hunting season, an additional 15 guides, three from each village, are employed to accompany safari hunting operators to monitor hunting activities to make sure that companies abide by their contract agreement.

Participation in ecotourism development has played a role in restructuring community capital dynamics, as the community now has a voice, makes decisions, earns financial gains, and collaborates and networks with different tourism stakeholders.

Changes in community needs

Based on the interviews and secondary data, it is apparent that changes in community needs can be explained by prevalence of cash flow, and transformation of agriculture.

Prevalence of cash flow

Due to participation in ecotourism, the prevalence of cash flow has contributed to changes in community needs. In all five villages, the cash economy has led to changing housing structures, from traditional housing made of mud, poles, and grass to more modern housing made of cement bricks, corrugated iron sheets, and windows. The transition to modern housing is attributed to money earned through ecotourism and from other sources not necessarily ecotourism related.

The change, as highlighted by most female household respondents, is also facilitated by restrictions imposed on the harvesting of certain resources, such as poles and thatching grass, within the buffer zone at certain times of the year. The need to continuously maintain traditional houses also makes them expensive to retain. The affordability of modern housing is the result of wages earned from tourism. Other services sought by the community include electricity, televisions, cars, radios, and mobile phones. One female Kachikau resident, age 33, remarked:

> before I started to work at Ngoma Lodge, I was unable to buy myself what I wanted, but today I have a better house, a cellphone, and I am able to buy better food as I have money to spend, unlike when I was unemployed.

Results further indicate that the financial capital accrued from ecotourism investments has helped the community to hire professionals (e.g. CECT's manager, accountant, and programme officer) to enhance the community's human capital. The financial capital also funds local activities that support cultural capital. For instance, five local cultural dance groups have been supported financially and were able to buy dancing regalia. Six groups engaged in handicrafts production have also benefited. The traditional dance and handicraft groups promote the cultural self-confidence and identity of the CECT community. Finances from ecotourism therefore boosted the preservation and transmission of cultural traits and traditions, safeguarding the community's heritage and revitalising local culture. Furthermore, the presence of tourists facilitated staged performances, restoring the community's cultural capital. Tourism has helped the CECT community realise the financial importance of the CNP and has infused a feeling of pride.

Financial gain has also brought changes in community needs, opening the community to cultural commoditisation and commercialisation. The presence of tourists and the promise of more income have encouraged the proliferation of arts and craft groups. Due to changes in community needs, the acquisition and accumulation of financial gain is given more priority than producing arte-facts that serve cultural purposes. Artefacts are priced in US dollars, an indi-cation that the target market is international tourists. The commercialisation of community cultural artefacts has some implications on the natural capital that supplies the community with souvenir materials because they are produced predominantly from a few selected plant species. Interviews with the DWNP official revealed that some community members enter the CNP illegally just for harvesting raw materials for souvenirs.

The commoditisation of culture manifests itself with the rejuvenation and packaging of cultural events and festivals. However, this development has changed the cultural assemblage and the environment in which these perform-ances take place; they can now be performed anytime and anywhere when the need arises.

The transformation of natural resources into a commodity started with the demarcation of land into hunting and photographic zones, a development related to the enclosure of spaces and the battling of control by guarding against other resource users who may want to benefit from the same resources. In the process, the community has gained political and social capital by showing high natural resource control, domination, and power. The wildlife has also become a commodity, sold to the highest bidding safari companies. A Kavimba male resident, age 41, remarked:

> All wild animals found in CH1 and CH2 are CECT's property, and depending on the quota we receive, we gain by selling them to highest bidding hunting safari companies.

CECT is a new institution that now has the authority and legitimacy to control wildlife by selling it at competitive prices to accumulate more financial capital. Wildlife in CNP is now viewed as a commodity that the community can sell to improve its livelihood.

Transformation of agriculture

The financial gains from ecotourism have facilitated the acquisition of six trac-tors with trailers and ploughing equipment, consequently improving arable farming, which further contributes to the community's physical capital. The introduction of tractors has led to the mechanisation of farming, transforming the agricultural landscape in terms of the total area ploughed and yields har-vested. Before participation in ecotourism, traditional farming methods were used to till the soil, leading to less hectares being ploughed and low yields being harvested. Records from the Ministry of Agriculture's Department of Crop Production (Botswana, 2012) indicate that there have been changes in the size of land tilled and crop yields (see Table 4).

Table 4 shows that between the years 2005/2006 and 2011/2012 (before and after the introduction of tractors), tilled land increased by 1574.98 ha, indicating that tractors have had an impact on agriculture. During the same period, there was a significant increase in terms of production (556.13 kg/ha more in yields) and the number of community beneficiaries (467 more community members benefitted).

CECT subsidises the use of the tractors to allow all members to have access to tractor services. Household interviews also indicate that some households that had given up farming due to lack of draught power are now ploughing due to the availability of tractors. A female Satau resident, age 58, remarked:

> Who would not appreciate the tractors that have relieved us; even those who had stopped plowing due to shortage of draught power are now active farmers. New farms and the farms that had been abandoned are now plowed.

Results also indicate that increases in the ploughing area have also increased human–wildlife conflicts. Table 4 shows that as the area ploughed increases, the area destroyed by wildlife also increases. The data and the interviews suggest that an increase in land tilling has improved the community food security while at the same time aggravating human–wildlife conflicts. The availability of tractors has resulted in a dire need for more land for ploughing. Even land not suitable for ploughing is now being occupied. For instance, between the years 2008/2009 and 2011/2012, a total of 382.93 hectares of land that was ploughed was flooded and the community lost its harvest (see Table 4). The crop flooding frequency rate is now higher than before the introduction of tractors, indicating that crop farming is colonising land that is vulnerable to flooding. Due to the availability of tractors, tilled land is increasing every ploughing season, resulting in more human–wildlife conflicts, which may negatively affect wildlife pathways.

While most ploughing fields are located on the Chobe River flood plains, most tourism and residential plots are located along the river bank making it difficult for wild animals to access the river water as wildlife corridors are restrained, and even blocked. To mitigate human–wildlife conflicts, some farmers have responded by fencing farmland. Interviews with DWNP and DCP officials indicate that fencing not only blocks wildlife corridors, but wild animals get tangled in the fence and get hurt or killed. However, it was determined from household interviews that elephants are not deterred by fencing,

Table 4. Total land ploughed and crop production output from 2006 to 2012.

Year	Area ploughed (ha)	Area planted (ha)	Yield (kg/ha)	Beneficiaries	Area (ha) lost to wildlife damage	Area (ha) lost to flooding
2005/2006	556.90	556.90	223.64	222	*	*
2006/2007	869.97	869.97	272.00	231	*	11.31
2007/2008	990.12	990.12	483.13	503	*	11.89
2008/2009	1524.19	1524.19	262.33	580	446.56	57.84
2009/2010	1800.69	1795.12	593.93	601	472.48	136.87
2010/2011	1873.33	1788.47	638.98	654	497.19	188.22
2011/2012	2131.88	2178.88	789.77	689	*	*

Source: Botswana (2012).
*Missing data.

in fact they destroy it to gain access to both the ploughing fields and the river water. This has fuelled more human–wildlife conflicts. For those with the means, electric fences have been erected to stop the intrusions.

Discussion

By adopting a case study approach and situating our analysis within the CCF, we were able to create a more holistic base through a systems thinking perspective in assessing how enhancements in community capital through ecotourism have influenced changes in community needs that in turn have influenced the functions of PAs. Hence, the framework is important for understanding and identifying asymmetries in capital flow and accumulation in evaluating the relationships among ecotourism, PAs and changes in livelihoods. The findings provide insights into the dynamics of biodiversity conservation and community development which are essential to researchers, planners, and policy-makers in their quest to devise adaptability measures in PAs. The enhancement of community capitals through tourism has brought multiple and multi-scalar drivers of change in community needs at both community and household levels.

First, the recognition of the essence of organising social capital among participating villages to form CECT and the coordination among stakeholders such as NGOs, donors, and government agencies was a very crucial starting point. Social capital has been proposed as the 'missing link' in development (Gutierrez-Montes, Emery, & Fernandez-Baca, 2009; Jones, 2005). The organisation of social capital led to social relations that led to constructive outcomes for the CECT project. The core idea of social capital is that social networks have value, as interaction and connections develop shared norms, trust, and reciprocity that in turn foster cooperation to achieve common ends (Molyneux, 2002). This, in turn, cultivated an environment conducive for the community's political will to embrace ecotourism development as a livelihood option. The external assistance through NGOs and donor funding agencies bridged the community's financial capital deficit. External public funding for tourism is crucial in rural areas where residents do not have sufficient incomes by themselves (Bennett, Lemelin, Kosterb, & Budke, 2012). The improved social, political, and financial capitals' interdependence provided the foundation to influence the community's utilisation of the cultural and natural capitals as forms of tourism attractions. In turn, the financial capital gained from tourism was invested in securing the human capital (hiring CECT professionals) and physical capital (tractors, lodge, and shops).

Furthermore, agricultural intensification financed by funds from tourism facilitated the mechanisation of farming and necessitated the need for more ploughing land, escalating the need to recover land appropriated for biodiversity conservation. Interestingly, though the community has substantially benefitted from ecotourism, this has not necessarily led to conservation support or action because the natural capital in the form of wildlife has destroyed the community's agriculture (physical capital). As in line with Christ (2003), investing ecotourism benefits to expand agriculture increases the threat to biodiversity. Relying on the 'cause effect' or unidirectional theoretical underpinnings (e.g. Berkes, 2004; Budowski, 1976; Carter, 1994), the expectation is that benefits from ecotourism will directly incentivise conservation creating positive linkages between PAs and communities. However, because the same ecotourism resources (wildlife) turn around and destroy community physical capital, positive linkage is not created.

Tourism has progressively opened the CNP natural capital to the outside world, creating a challenge for the park to deal with the growing interest of outsiders. This has introduced a model where natural resources are exchanged in an exploitative manner for financial and physical capitals gain. The introduction of cash flow in a rural and isolated area facilitates changes in community needs and triggers community transformation, producing environmental consequences which need further mitigation interventions.

While ecotourism development can be credited with contributing to improved livelihoods at CECT, it can also be blamed for accelerating changes in community needs. In this regard, the sustainability of PAs in the long-term becomes questionable. A greater challenge perhaps is the reconciliation between the effects of changing community needs and PAs' biodiversity conservation objectives. However, the call for more systems thinking approaches, as condoned by the CCF, endorse these approaches that are system discerning by encapsulating social, cultural, financial, political, natural, human, and physical aspects of the setting in defining the assets' stock and flow of a system. Therefore, diverse variable assessments and links are considered key, so change efforts are not centred on only one productive activity but all that are related. Recognising the failure of past tourism approaches in addressing both the upswing in poverty and environmental degradation, this study encourages the adoption of evaluation approaches enshrined on systems-level destination capitals perspectives in future research and practice than on 'cause effects' domains.

The essence of the CCF may help individuals understand the adaptive capacity, or vulnerability status of communities and PAs' biodiversity, as the relationship between community livelihoods and PAs is not static but dynamic. The level and patterns of livelihood diversification demonstrate that the community adaptive capacity may be sufficient for current community livelihoods practices, but may be inadequate in the future as community livelihoods and needs continue changing.

A big challenge in adaptive management is that community change and PAs' biodiversity have been observed as distinct and unrelated issues (Wilson, 1992). The challenge for PA tourism is not the absence of any resulting negative impacts, but rather the on-going intent by managers to pursue sustainability outcomes in line with the best available knowledge, and to quickly and effectively address any negative impacts that inadvertently arise from tourism core activities (Weaver, 2002).

This study recognises that as long as we are living in social systems, a transformation or substitution among the various forms of community capitals is unavoidable. Therefore, we must be vigilant in remembering the dangers that arise from our human tendency to engage in short term and geographically bounded thinking. This form of thinking encourages decision-makers to overly expense other forms of capital for relatively short-term economic gain, henceforth, causing imbalances in view of other forms of capitals. Roberts and Hall (2001) noted that policy-makers sometimes have a tendency to think of tourism development without necessarily accounting for the physical, cultural, social, political, economic, and ecological contexts for rural development processes. Applying the systems thinking approach on evaluating ecotourism projects' contribution to conservation and development could be a good policy communication device for all stakeholders involved in community-ecotourism projects.

Conclusion

This study explored how the development of ecotourism has influenced changes in community needs and the functions of PAs using the CCF. As the community's financial capital gained through ecotourism allowed them to invest more in agriculture, it created some unintended consequences, including more demand of agriculture land and heightening community–wildlife conflicts. The findings challenged the unidimensional approach of ecotourism project to improve the livelihood and enhance biodiversity conservation goals. This paper makes two major contributions to the conservation-development and sustainable tourism literature. First, the utility of systems thinking is that development should not only be equated with economic growth as the only indicator of interest, at the same time, high level of biodiversity integrity alone should not be the only indicator, because economic growth and high levels of biodiversity integrity cannot be realised at the detriment of the other, but need other forms of capitals. It is the system interdependence offered by realising the importance of all community capitals helps researchers to evaluate the performance of the overall Pas' ecosystem. Thus, to evaluate the role of one form of capital in isolation of others would limit our understanding of the role they play in tourism development and conservation nexus.

Second, as the relationship between PAs, tourism and community livelihoods is dynamic, change is inevitable; therefore, the inevitability for change can be analysed by locating trends and going through a learning process vis-à-vis the system on which tourism and community livelihoods operate to devise adaptive management mechanisms. The importance of understanding the role of ecotourism's contribution to community's needs changes through systems thinking approach research, which constitutes a useful foundation for enhancing higher order thinking in addressing complex real world problems (Becken, 2013), and transcends traditional epistemologies that characterises tourism research (Tribe & Xiao, 2011). It should be in the minds of conservation-development agents that the attraction of a simple solution to complex intractable problems is obvious, but the likelihood of finding a magic bullet is probably low (Botterill & Fisher, 2002). Benefitting from this research, future studies could re-visit PAs policies to reassess their evolution towards sustainability. As the wave of accommodating tourism by PAs moves forward, it will be of importance to closely monitor and evaluate not only its advancement, but also how PAs and communities incorporate change.

As a limitation of the study, the indicators, components, and capitals were all weighted equally at each stage of the framework leading to the final analysis. However, it is likely that the relative importance of each capital varies significantly. As a recommendation, further research can be geared towards the application and expansion of the framework by ranking and weighting the community capitals.

Disclosure statement

No potential conflict of interest was reported by the authors.

References

Aigner, S. M., Flora, C. B., & Hernandez, J. M. (2001). The premise and promise of citizenship and civil society for renewing democracies and empowering sustainable communities. *Sociological Inquiry, 71*, 493–507.

Alkire, S. (2002). Dimensions of human development. *World Development, 30*(2), 181–205.

Altman, J., & Finlayson, J. (1993). Aborigines, tourism and sustainable development. *Journal of Tourism Studies, 4*(1), 38–50.

Anon. (1991). *Chambers Concise English Dictionary.* Edinburgh: W&R Chambers.

Ashley, C., & Elliott, J. (2003). 'Just wildlife?'or a source of local development?. *ODI Natural resource perspectives,* (85). Retrieved from https://www.odi.org/sites/odi.org.uk/files/odi-assets/publications-opinion-files/2790.pdf

Bebbington, A. (1999). Capitals and capabilities: A framework for analyzing peasant viability, rural livelihoods and poverty. *World Development, 27*(12), 2021–2044.

Becken, S. (2013). Developing a framework for assessing resilience of tourism sub-systems to climatic factors. *Annals of Tourism Research, 43*, 506–528.

Bennett, N., Lemelin, H., Kosterb, R., & Budke, I. (2012). A capital assets framework for appraising and building capacity for tourism development in aboriginal protected area gateway communities. *Tourism Management, 33*, 752–766.

Berkes, F. (2004). Rethinking community-based conservation. *Conservation Biology, 18*(3), 621–630.

Bernard, H., & Ryan, G. (2003). Techniques to identify themes in qualitative data. *Field Methods, 15*(1), 85–109.

Boggs, L. P. (2001). *Community power, participation, conflict and development choice: Community wildlife conservation in the Okavango Region of Northern Botswana* (Discussion Paper No. 17). Maun, Botswana: IIED.

Botswana. (2011). *Botswana population & housing census.* Gaborone: Government Printers.

Botswana. (2012). *ISPAAD weekly report.* Kasane: Chobe Crop Production Office.

Botterill, C., & Fisher, M. (2002). *Magical thinking: The rise of the community participation model.* A paper presented to the Jubilee conference of the Australasian Political Studies Association. Canberra: Australian National University.

Bramwell, B., & Lane, B. (2013). Getting from here to there: Systems change, behavioural change and sustainable tourism. *Journal of Sustainable Tourism, 21*(1), 1–4.

Budowski, G. (1976). Tourism and environmental conservation: Conflict, coexistence, or symbiosis? *Environmental Conservation, 3,* 27–31.

Butler, R. (1999). Sustainable tourism: A state of the art review. *Tourism Geographies, 1*(1), 7–25.

Carter, E. (1994). Introduction. In E. Cater & G. Lowman (Eds.), *Ecotourism: A sustainable option?* (pp. 3–16). New York, NY: Wiley.

CECT. (2011). *Annual general meeting minutes.* Kavimba.

Charmaz, K. (2006). *Constructing grounded theory: A practical guide through qualitative research.* London: Sage Publications.

Christ, C. (2003). *Tourism and biodiversity: Mapping tourism's global footprint.* Washington, DC: Conservation International.

Deneulin. S. (2008). Beyond individual freedom and agency: Structures of living together in the capability approach. In F. Comim, M. Qizilbash & S. Alkire (Eds.), *The capability approach: Concepts, Measures and Applications* (pp. 105–124). Cambridge: Cambridge University Press.

Denzin, N., & Lincoln, Y. (2000). *Handbook of qualitative research* (2nd ed.). Thousand Oaks, CA: Sage.

De Sherbinin, A., VanWey, L. K., McSweeney, K., Aggarwal, R., Barbieri, A., Henry, S., ... & Walker, R. (2008). Rural household demographics, livelihoods and the environment. *Global Environmental Change, 18*(1), 38–53.

Emery, M., Fey, S., & Flora, C. (2006). *Using community capitals to develop assets for positive community change Practice.* Retrieved September 3, 2013, from http://www.commdev.org/index.php?option=com_content&view=article&id=70& Itemid

Farrell, B., & Twining-Ward, L. (2004). Reconceptualizing tourism. *Annals of Tourism Research, 31*(2), 274–295.

Fey, S., Bregendahl, C., & Flora, C. (2006). The measurement of community capitals through research. *Online Journal of Rural Research & Policy, 1*(1), 1. doi:10.4148/ojrrp.v1i1.29

Fiallo, A., & Jacobson, S. (1995). Local communities and protected areas: Attitudes of rural residents towards conservation and Machalilla National Park, Ecuador. *Environmental Conservation, 22*(3), 241–249.

Flora, C. (2005). Social aspects of small water systems. *Journal of Contemporary Water Research, 126,* 6–12.

Flora, C., & Emery, M. (2006). Spiraling-up: Mapping community transformation with community capitals framework. *Community Development, 37*(1), 19–35.

Flora, C., Flora, J., & Fey, S. (2004). *Rural communities: Legacy and change* (2nd ed.). Boulder, CO: Westview Press.

Forrester, J. W. (1961). *Industrial dynamics.* Cambridge: MIT Press.

Ghimire, K., & Pimbert, M. (1997). Social change and conservation: An overview of issues and concepts. In K. Ghimire & M. Pimbert (Eds.), *Social change and conservation:*

Environmental politics and impacts of national parks and protected areas (pp. 1–45). London: Earthscan.

Gossling, S., Hall, C., & Weaver, D. (Eds.). (2009). *Sustainable tourism futures. Perspectives on systems, restructuring and innovations*. New York, NY: Routledge.

Gossling, S., Hall, C., Ekstrom, F., Engeset, A., & Aall, C. (2012). Transition management: A tool for implementing sustainable tourism scenarios? *Journal of Sustainable Tourism, 20* (6), 899–916.

Gutierrez-Montes, I., Emery, M., & Fernandez-Baca, E. (2009). The sustainable livelihoods approach and the community capitals framework: The importance of system-level approaches to community change efforts. *Community Development, 40*(2), 106–113.

Hall, M. (2011). Policy learning and policy failure in sustainable tourism governance: From first- and second-order to third-order change? *Journal of Sustainable Tourism, 9*(5), 649–671.

Harrison, J., MacGibbon, L., & Morton, M. (2001). Regimes of trustworthiness in qualitative research: The rigors of reciprocity. *Qualitative Inquiry, 7*(3), 323–345.

Heinen, J. (1993). Park–people relations in Kosi Tappu Wildlife Reserve, Nepal: A socio-economic analysis. *Environmental Conservation, 20*(1), 25–34.

Holling, C., & Chambers, A. (1973). Resource science: The nurture of an infant. *BioScience, 23*(1), 13–20.

Holmberg, A., & Dobyns, H. (1962). The process of accelerating community change. *Human Organizations, XXI*, 107–109.

Hunter, C. (1997). Sustainable tourism as an adaptive paradigm. *Annals of Tourism Research, 24*, 850–867.

IUCN. (1994). *Guidelines for protected area management categories*. Gland: Author.

Jacobs, C. (2007). *Measuring success in communities: Understanding the community capitals framework*. Community Capitals Series # 1, Extension Extra. South Dakota State University, Vermillion, Cooperative Extension Service.

Jones, B. (2002). *Chobe Enclave, Botswana – Lessons learnt from a CBNRM project 1993–2002*. Gaborone: Bay.

Jones, B. (2003). *CBNRM in Botswana: Review of the tender assessment process for community controlled hunting areas*. Washington, DC: Chemonics International.

Jones, S. (2005). Community-based ecotourism: The significance of social capital. *Annals of Tourism Research, 32*(2), 303–324.

Laverack, G., & Wallerstein, N. (2001). Measuring community empowerment: A fresh look at organizational domains. *Health Promotion International, 16*(2), 179–185.

Lenao, M. (2013). Challenges facing community-based cultural tourism development at Lekhubu Island, Botswana: A comparative analysis. *Current Issues in Tourism*, 1–16. doi:10.1080/13683500.2013.827158

Lieblich, A., Tuval-Mashiach, R., & Zilber, T. (1998). *Narrative research: Reading, analysis and interpretation*. Newbury Park, CA: Sage.

Lippett, R., Jeannie, W., & Bruce, W. (1958). *The dynamics of planned change: A comparative study of principles and techniques*. New York, NY: Harcourt, Brace & World.

Mbaiwa, J. (2011). The effects of tourism development on the sustainable utilisation of natural resources in the Okavango Delta, Botswana. *Current Issues in Tourism, 14*(3), 251–273.

Mbaiwa, J., & Stronza, A. (2011). The effects of tourism development on rural livelihoods in the Okavango Delta, Botswana. *Journal of Sustainable Tourism, 18*(5), 35–56.

Miles, M., & Huberman, A. (1994). *Qualitative data analysis*. Thousand Oaks, CA: Sage.

Molyneux, M. (2002). Gender and silences of social capital: Lessons from Latin America. *Development and Change, 33*, 167–188.

Moser, W., & Petersen, J. (1981). Limits to Obergurgl's growth: Alpine experience in environmental management. *Ambio, 10*(2), 68–72.

Moxley, R. (1985). Vertical assistance, population size and growth in the context and results of community civic action. *Journal of Community Development, 16*(1), 57–167.

Naughton-Treves, L., Holland, M., & Brandon, K. (2005). The role of protected areas in conserving biodiversity and sustaining local livelihoods. *Annual Review of Environment and Resources, 30*, 219–252.

Nchunga, C. (2003). *Background formation and progress of the CECT.* Kasane: Chobe Enclave Conservation Trust.

Nyaupane, G. P., & Poudel, S. (2011). Linkages among biodiversity, livelihood, and tourism. *Annals of Tourism Research, 38*(4), 1344–1366.

Padgett, D. (2008). *Qualitative methods in social work research.* Thousand Oaks, CA: Sage.

Patton, M. (1990). *Qualitative evaluation and research methods.* Newbury Park, CA: Sage.

Portes, A. (2000, March). The two meanings of social capital. *Sociological Forum, 15*(1) 1–12.

Roberts, L., & Hall, D. (2001). *Rural tourism and recreation: Principles and practice.* Wallingford: CABI.

Saarinen, J., & Lenao, M. (2014). Integrating tourism to rural development and planning in the developing world. *Development Southern Africa, 31*(3), 363–372.

Saayman, M., & Saayman, A. (2006). Estimating the economic contribution of visitor spending in the Krugar National Park to the regional economy. *Journal of Sustainable Tourism, 14* (1), 67–81.

Saggers, S. (2003). Measuring community development: Perspectives from local government in Western Australia. *Australian Journal of Social Issues, 38*(1), 5–23.

Salafsky, N., & Wollenberg, E. (2000). Linking livelihoods and conservation: A conceptual framework and scale for assessing the integral of human needs and biodiversity. *World Development, 28*(8), 1421–1438.

Sanders, I. (1958). *The community: An introduction to a social system.* New York, NY: Ronald Press.

Sanderson, S. (2005). Poverty and conservation: The new century's 'peasant question'. *World Development, 33*(2), 323–332.

Sekhar, N. (2003). Local people's attitudes towards conservation and wildlife tourism around Sariska Tiger Reserve, India. *Journal of Environmental Management, 69*, 339–347.

Sen, A. (2009). *The idea of justice.* London: Peguin.

Serageldin, I., & Steer, A. (1994). Epilogue: Expanding the capital stock. In I. Serageldin & A. Steer (Eds.), *Making development sustainable: From concepts to action* (pp. 224–140). Washington, DC: World Bank.

Sharpley, R. (2009). *Tourism development and the environment: Beyond sustainability?* Sterling, VA: Earthscan.

Sterman, D. (2002). *System dynamics: Systems thinking and modeling for a complex world.* Working Paper Series. ESD-WP-2003-01.13-ESD Internal Symposium. Cambridge: Massachusetts Institute of Technology Engineering Systems Division.

Stone, L. S., & Stone, M. T. (2011). Community-based tourism enterprises: Challenges and prospects for community participation; Khama Rhino Sanctuary Trust, Botswana. *Journal of Sustainable Tourism, 19*, 97–114.

Stone, M. T., & Nyaupane, G. P. (2016). Protected areas, tourism and community livelihoods linkages: A comprehensive analysis approach. *Journal of Sustainable Tourism, 24*(5), 673–693.

Strickland-Munro, J., Allison, H., & Moore, A. (2010). Using resilience concepts to investigate the impacts of protected area tourism on communities. *Annals of Tourism Research, 37*(2), 499–519.

Summers, G. (1986). Rural community development. *Annual Review of Sociology, 12*, 347–371.

Swarbrooke, J. (1999). *Sustainable tourism management*. Oxon: CABI.

Tribe, J., & Xiao, H. (2011). Developments in tourism and social science editorial. *Annals of Tourism Research, 38*(1), 7–26.

Walker, P., Greiner, R., McDonald, D., & Lyne, V. (1998). The tourism futures simulator: A systems thinking approach. *Environmental Modelling & Software, 14* (1), 59–67.

Walpole, M., & Goodwin, H. (2001). Local attitudes towards conservation and tourism around Komodo National Park, Indonesia. *Environmental Conservation, 28*(2), 160–166.

Weaver, D. (2002). *Ecotourism*. Brisbane: Wiley.

Wilson, E. O. (1992). *The diversity of life*. New York, NY: Norton.

The role of private sector ecotourism in local socio-economic development in southern Africa

Susan Snyman

ABSTRACT

Ecotourism is frequently put forward as a potential solution for local development and biodiversity conservation in developing countries. Numerous researchers have looked at the various impacts of ecotourism on development and on conservation. There are, however, few studies looking at the role of stakeholders and the impact they are having on local development. We look specifically at the role of private sector stakeholders in local ecotourism development in southern Africa. We focus on one ecotourism operator, Wilderness Safaris, and our results are based on a desktop analysis of various reports, field work and data from a Ph.D. study looking at the socio-economic impact of private sector ecotourism on local communities. The results show that the private sector has an important role to play in local socio-economic development in terms of employment creation, skills training and development, the payment of lease fees as well as through philanthropic development projects. Recommendations are put forward as to how the private sector can further effect positive change in the areas where it is operating and ensure long-term sustainability.

1. Introduction

Ecotourism development in remote, rural areas in southern Africa has become synonymous with local socio-economic development and is in some cases seen as a panacea (Akama & Kieti, 2007; Binns & Nel, 2002; Briedenhann & Wickens, 2004; Kavita & Saarinen, 2015). It is not a panacea, but it certainly can play an important role in terms of poverty reduction and local socio-economic development (Snyman, 2012b, 2013, 2014c; Spenceley & Goodwin, 2007). This paper focuses specifically on the role of private sector ecotourism in southern African in terms of its potential impact on local socio-economic development.

Over the years, African governments and state conservation departments have been turning to the private sector to assist with the management and maintenance of conservation areas (Spenceley, 2003), as it seems better placed to identify opportunities, realise the potential of a destination, drive forward product development and implement effective strategies to benefit communities' livelihoods (Simpson, 2008). This article presents aspects of research conducted in six southern African countries (Botswana, Malawi, Namibia, South Africa, Zambia and Zimbabwe), as well as data collected through various annual Integrated Reports and the author's experiences in the field.

Past research has looked at different impacts of tourism, including negative and positive socio-economic impacts (Ahebwa, van der Duim, & Sandbrook, 2011; Andereck, Valentine, Knopf, & Vogt, 2005; Fennell, 2008; Goodwin, 2008; Mitchell & Ashley, 2010; Novelli & Scarth, 2007; Snyman, 2012a, 2012b; Stronza & Pêgas, 2008; Telfer & Sharpley, 2008), sociocultural impacts (Ashley, Goodwin, & Roe, 2001; Eagles, McCool, & Haynes, 2002; Mbaiwa, 2003; Snyman, 2012a; Telfer & Sharpley, 2008) and environmental impacts (Andereck et al., 2005; Mbaiwa, 2003; Stronza, 2010; Telfer & Sharpley, 2008). Although it is clear that ecotourism can introduce costs and benefits to local communities, the role of the private sector in this has not been adequately addressed. The policy implication is simple; ecotourism is becoming an increasingly complex phenomenon, with political, economic, social, cultural, educational, ecological, psychological and aesthetic dimensions. In rural areas, ecotourism's sustainability will, therefore, have to provide benefits to communities as a means of motivating and enabling residents to care for and maintain their natural and cultural heritage, often viewed at the ecotourism product.

There is currently little literature focusing on the specific roles of stakeholders in ecotourism, particularly the private sector. There has been discussion about the various potential partnerships between the private sector and communities (Snyman, 2013, 2014b; Spenceley, 2003) and between the private sector and governments through public–private partnerships (Varghese, 2008), but little discussion of the potential roles that the private sector can and does play in terms of local development. Bond et al. (2004) looked at the role of private sector land contribution to conservation in South Africa, but not at development impacts. This paper aims to fill this gap in the literature.

Defining ecotourism and its relationship to conservation is contextually important to this study. There are numerous definitions of ecotourism that have developed over the years (see Blamey, 1997; Ceballos-Lascuráin, 1996; Fennell, 2001, 2008). The term 'ecotourism' was claimed to be originally coined by Ceballos-Lascuráin in 1983, but more recently, Fennell (2008, p. 24) defined ecotourism as

a sustainable, non-invasive form of nature-based tourism that focuses primarily on learning about nature first-hand, and which is ethically managed to be low-impact, non-consumptive, and locally oriented (control, benefits, scale). It typically occurs in natural areas, and should contribute to the conservation of such areas.

Fennell's definition of ecotourism as non-consumptive, therefore, excludes hunting or fishing as ecotourism options. This is restrictive and leans more towards the protectionist or preservationist viewpoint rather than mere conservation.

In summarising the literature, De Witt, van der Merwe, and Saayman (2011, p. 1139) suggest that the key principles of ecotourism are that it should foster a genuine interest in nature, contribute to conservation, respect and conserve local culture, make non-consumptive use of natural resources, yield benefits to the local community and create tourist awareness of conservation and local community issues. Agrawal and Redford (2006) suggest the following two core criteria: it should generate low visitor impact and help to conserve biodiversity; and it should generate beneficial socio-economic outcomes for local people to help in poverty reduction. Based on these definitions, ecotourism in this paper is taken to include activities that are nature- and culture-based, sustainable, promote conservation and provide benefits to local people in the area (Snyman, 2014c). It is therefore not simply tourism that is based on the sale of access to an interesting natural area, but tourism that also provides benefits to local communities. Since many of the impacts, costs and benefits of tourism are the same as those for ecotourism in the study areas, the two terms are used synonymously throughout the paper. This paper focuses specifically on the role of private sector ecotourism in the provision of benefits as per ecotourism's definition.

1.1. Role of ecotourism

The role of ecotourism in local socio-economic development has been credited with providing benefits such as employment opportunities and capacity building through skills training and development programmes; payment of lease fees; creation of joint ventures (JVs) and other partnerships; development of local linkages/value chains; infrastructure development as well as philanthropic donations (Snyman, 2013). This paper will look at private sector ecotourism's role in a number of these areas.

Despite its theorised benefits, there has been much debate regarding the 'leakage' from tourism operations in rural areas, specifically from private sector ecotourism (Mbaiwa, 2003). Meyer (2008, p. 561) defines leakage as the percentage of the price of a holiday paid by tourists that either leaves the destination in payment for imports or as expatriated profits, or that never reaches the destination due to the involvement of foreign intermediaries. Leakages can be identified and measured by assessing the supply of goods and services that are being imported to fill market needs and, from there, looking for local alternatives (see Figure 1), which have an obvious impact on local socio-economic development.

Sandbrook (2010) argues that although there was a considerable amount of leakage from his Ugandan study sites in villages around Bwindi Impenetrable Forest, the retained revenue was still greater than all other sources of revenue

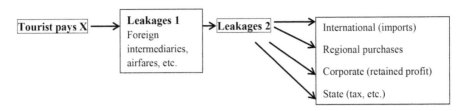

Figure 1. Leakages from tourism.

to the area combined. He therefore argues that the knock-on effects of tourism, in the local context, can be highly significant despite considerable leakage. Investments in local socio-economic development, such as infrastructure, may also be more important locally than the impact of leakages.

The private sector is oriented towards generating revenue and profit from selling tourism products and services (Spenceley, 2003). There are, however, indications that the private sector is also playing an increasingly important role in conservation and local socio-economic development (Spenceley, 2003). The private sector has capital available for the development of new tourism ventures, as well as marketing capabilities, greater advertising opportunities, economies of scale and financial management skills (Spenceley, 2003).

1.2. Ecotourism stakeholders

Numerous stakeholders participate in ecotourism including the private sector, non-governmental organisations (NGOs), government, local communities, support institutions, universities and researchers. Their differing roles depend on the particular form of ecotourism and the level of participation required. Table 1 summarises various interactions observed between three of the main stakeholders engaging in a private sector ecotourism operation (adapted from Currie, 2001, in Snyman, 2013).

Private sector ecotourism operators may choose to engage in a partnership with a community for a variety of reasons. Spenceley (2003) lists a number of reasons over and above the pure profit motive: obligations to provide benefits to rural communities through concession arrangements, the diversification of commercial activities, driven by Corporate Social Responsibility and image; or market advantage. Ashley and Roe (2002) emphasised that when engaging with communities, the private sector does endure certain costs that go beyond simple financial costs to include problems of time, uncertainty and risk. Armstrong (2012) stresses that if engagements with communities are to be successful, the private sector operator needs to be ethically responsible and prepared to make a long-term commitment to the community and its development. Its investment in ecotourism is also affected by other stakeholders who are identified and discussed in the remainder of this section.

Table 1. Role of major stakeholders.

	Conservation	Tourism	Community members
Conservation (often National Parks/ Government, but can also be communal)		Ensure good wildlife-viewing Ensure natural habitats for tourism Provide necessary infrastructure such as roads, etc. Provide anti-poaching measures to increase wildlife numbers	Mitigate human–wildlife conflict Allow for sustainable natural resource utilisation Provide community environmental education Involve local community members in decision-making that affects their lives
Tourism	Sustainable development which minimises negative environmental impacts Provide revenues for resource protection Raise and manage funds for conservation projects Maintain areas as conservation, rather than other land uses		Equitably share individual and collective tourism revenues Involve community members in tourism, through employment, partnerships and supply chains Ensure tourist respect for local cultures Broaden benefit-sharing options
Community members	Participate in anti-poaching Adhere to resource use restrictions Promote and support conservation in the area	Involvement in tourism through employment, village visits, supply chain and partnerships Welcome tourists and ensure their safety Integrate culture into tourism	

Source: Snyman (2013).

Because of the remote nature of many ecotourism operations, communities are important stakeholders, frequently supplying land, resources and labour. Communities are not homogenous, but are constantly changing, defining and redefining themselves, their needs and their aspirations (Boissevan, 1996 as cited in Jones, 2001; Novelli & Scarth, 2007; Telfer & Sharpley, 2008). Their component groups are distinguished by age, gender, ethnicity and socio-economic status and all these groups compete for the rights, revenues and resources available (Jones, 2001, p. 173). At the start of any tourism development, communities should be identified, as should their boundaries, membership, roles, responsibilities, attitudes and socio-economic needs (Jones, 2001). A plan for the distribution and management of any benefits should be clearly set out. If this is not done, future conflicts are likely, jeopardising the long-term sustainability of local ecotourism and conservation as land uses (Snyman, 2014b).

Government is important as a provider of the infrastructure and institutions necessary to ensure private sector investment and commitment, as well as local support. It can create the appropriate conditions for private sector investment in ecotourism and local supply chains by providing support and incentivising investment. There are a number of different strategies for governments to engage in that can help to stimulate microenterprise, promote more business linkages and increase the number of benefits reaching the poor (see Ashley, 2006; De Boer, van Dijk, & Tarimo, 2011; Vedeld, Jumane, Wapalila, & Songorwa, 2012). Strategies include, amongst others, tax subsidies for businesses using local linkages, enabling legislation for microenterprises, etc.

There are numerous NGOs working in rural areas in southern Africa, such as the Integrated Rural Development and Nature Conservation (IRDNC), Namibian Association of CBNRM Organisations (NACSO), Save the Rhino Trust (SRT), World Wildlife Fund (WWF), African Safari Lodge Foundation (ASLF), Conservation International (CI) and others. These NGOs are involved in various activities including capacity building, conservation, education and consultancy. NGOs' role in developing community/tourism partnerships, through focusing on empowerment and building local capacity by means of training, education, organisational support and networking, is important, but there is a risk of unmet expectations.

Academic researchers can play an important role as providers of data and information to decision-makers in NGOs and other organisations trying to ensure the sustainability of ecotourism developments and engagements with local communities. It is important, however, that researchers are respectful towards communities, their culture, wishes and desires and that they do not unnecessarily impose themselves on local communities or use ill-conceived research questions that influence community views and cause discontent (Snyman, 2013). Epler Wood International (2004) suggest that local research institutions who partner with local businesses and build the capacity of students and professionals deliver cost-effective services to ecotourism by conducting important ecotourism research and capacity building.

Given the roles of the various stakeholders described above, the objectives of this study were to:

(1) Assess the possible roles of private sector ecotourism in positive local socio-economic development in southern Africa.
(2) Use Wilderness Safaris (WS), a private sector ecotourism company, as a case study to assess the potential socio-economic development impacts.
(3) To provide recommendations, based on the analysis and author's experience, to maximise local positive socio-economic developments to effect sustainable positive change.

2. Methods used in the study[1]

A single ecotourism enterprise, WS,[2] was used for this study. It was the only ecotourism company that had parallel ecotourism operations, operating according to a standard policy framework, over the six Anglophone countries in the region: Botswana, Malawi, Namibia, South Africa, Zambia and Zimbabwe. This epitomised the international scope of private sector ecotourism across southern Africa.

The use of a single company made for ease of comparison, since the head office imposes a consistent management style over its different camps in southern Africa. The company itself wished to quantify the impact of its ecotourism operations on rural communities, and gave the author access to its camps and staff and to the communities with whom they engage.

The results in this paper are based on a desktop analysis of WS's annual Integrated Report data, the author's field experience with WS over the past seven years, as well as data collected through a larger, more complex Ph.D. study. Although the author was employed by WS at the time of the study, the research was conducted as an independent researcher and was in no way directly influenced by the company. The bulk of the Ph.D. study was a quantitative analysis including rigorous statistical analyses to ensure objectivity and to reduce bias. Where qualitative analysis was included, it was largely direct quotes from respondents to ensure a fair representation of attitudes and opinions. The author has worked in ecotourism and community development in different areas for over 20 years and, therefore, had an understanding of the various issues involved prior to beginning the study. Although this could introduce bias based on past assumptions, it also resulted in a richer analysis and enhanced engagement during the interviews. The author tried to ensure that she had current background knowledge of the areas being researched and also engaged with local community members regularly to ensure that their point of view was incorporated in the study and taken into account in all analyses.

In the Ph.D. study, extensive interviews were conducted in over 30 rural communities in 6 southern African countries. In total, 1785 community interview schedules were conducted in ecotourism camps (385 staff) and rural villages (1400 non-staff) either within or adjacent to protected areas (PAs).[3] All respondents lived in, or adjacent to, the conservation area in which the ecotourism operation was situated. The interviews were conducted by both male and female interviewers, and local translators were used in circumstances where the respondent could not speak or understand English. The interview schedule consisted of a structured set of questions, with the majority being close-ended, and a few having the option for further explanation. The interview schedules contained questions relating to demographics, social welfare and living standards, education, employment patterns, income and expenses, health and safety, and attitudes towards tourism[4] and conservation. Each interview was conducted verbally, with the interviewer completing the interview schedule. Each interview took approximately 20–45 minutes depending on the respondent's educational level and whether or not translation was required. Staff and non-staff respondents were given the same interview schedules, except for a short section in the attitudes section where non-staff respondents had additional questions related to WS. Every effort was made to keep the interviews uniform and to ask questions in such a manner as to reduce bias or at least keep it consistent. In order to render any existing bias relatively constant, the author conducted over 1000 of the interviews herself. Eight other interviewers assisted across the six countries and were informally trained by the author. Data were analysed using SPSS version 12 and STATA version 11.2 and included descriptive statistical analysis as well as regression models and Probits.

Two types of community members were targeted in this study; those from the community employed in WS' ecotourism operation (staff) and those not employed in the ecotourism operation (non-staff). The selection of study sites was dictated by the presence of a community–ecotourism relationship or partnership, or because the community lived in or adjacent to the conservation or protected area, or a combination of these. Table 2 summarises the interview schedule totals.

The survey period of 22 months (from January 2009 to October 2010) incorporated both the pilot and the main study. The pilot interviews were conducted at Chintheche Inn overlooking Lake Malawi where 26 staff interviews were conducted. The interview schedule was then revised for the main study based on the pilot and on comments from respondents. One question was added and a few were revised to ensure clarity and consistency for the main study.

Although the camps and communities were diverse (with varying land management systems, ethnic groups and tourism camp price ranges), as only one ecotourism operator was included in the analysis, there could be limitations to the generalisability of the research. The sample size was not standardised in all study countries due to logistical constraints in some areas where communities were large. These differences in the percentage of the community interviewed could result in some issues relating to external validity. It was, however, felt that all sample sizes were sufficient in the areas surveyed and no new information was found after a certain percentage (approximately 100 households) of the community had been interviewed (Snyman, 2013).

In addition, as a result of the diversity in tourism camps, ethnic groups and different land management systems, issues of heterogeneity could be present. As the main aim of the Ph.D. study was to quantify the impacts of ecotourism employment per se, it was felt that these differences added qualitatively to the analysis and provided important analyses of comparisons between different areas and countries (Snyman, 2013).

Table 2. Total number of staff and non-staff interviews conducted in each country.

Country	Total staff interview	Total non-staff interview	Total number of interviews
Botswana	99	261	360
Malawi	74	251	325
Namibia	81	271	352
South Africa	61	329	390
Zambia	15	67	83[a]
Zimbabwe	55	221	276
Total	385	1400	1785

Source: Snyman (2013).
[a]Despite the small sample size in Zambia, it was felt to be relevant and representative of the area where the interviews were conducted.

3. Results

The results section is divided into six sections highlighting the main positive roles of private sector ecotourism in terms of local socio-economic development. There are obviously a number of areas where private sector ecotourism can have negative impacts on communities, including through negative sociocultural, environmental and economic impacts (Snyman, 2013). These are not discussed in this paper as the aim was to look at how private sector ecotourism can positively impact local socio-economic development. The negative impacts should, however, be taken into account when considering the development of ecotourism in an area.

3.1. Employment opportunities and capacity building

Employment in any form of ecotourism is one of its most important contributions to local socio-economic development (Mitchell & Ashley, 2010). The direct benefit of wages and salaries to household welfare goes beyond their contribution to incomes; it allows investment in productive assets and gives ecotourism staff future security as well as the opportunity to diversify their livelihoods (Snyman, 2013).

In 2014–2015, WS employed 2436 people across 7 southern African countries (Botswana, Malawi, Namibia, Seychelles, South Africa, Zambia and Zimbabwe), more than 70% of whom came from local rural communities (Wilderness Holdings, 2015). Table 3 illustrates the average number of people supported by ecotourism staff, highlighting the extensive reach of ecotourism employment and its wider, indirect impact. Across six of the southern African countries of operation, Snyman (2013) found that, on average, each ecotourism staff member was supporting seven people. This illustrates the conduit through which wages earned by a worker translate into welfare impacts for others in remote rural areas (Snyman, 2012b). Tourism also has the ability to employ unskilled labour (no previous permanent employment, see Table 4) as well as a number of women. This creates job opportunities for previously excluded people and is important in terms of equitable socio-economic development in remote areas ('inclusive growth'). Out of 385 ecotourism staff interviewed in 16 ecotourism camps in 6 southern African countries, 63% said that their current job in ecotourism

Table 3. Average number of dependents at each study site.

Country[a]	Staff ($n = 385$)	Non-staff ($n = 1359$)	Average ($n = 1744$)
Botswana	8.11 (min. 0, max. 22)	5.09 (min. 0, max. 36)	5.91 (min 0, max. 36)
Malawi	7.93 (min. 1, max. 19)	4.24 (min. 0, max. 17)	5.14 (min. 0, max. 19)
Namibia	6.05 (min.0, max. 15)	6.02 (min. 0, max. 100)	6.02 (min. 0, max. 100)
South Africa	6.16 (min. 1, max. 15)	3.85 (min. 0, max. 29)	4.22 (min. 0, max. 29)
Zambia	7.27 (min. 3, max. 12)	5.66 (min. 0, max. 20)	5.95 (min. 0, max. 20)
Zimbabwe	8.11 (min. 1, max. 18)	5.35 (min. 0, max. 17)	5.91 (min. 0, max. 18)
Average	7.30 (min. 0; max. 22)	4.9 (min. 0; max. 100)	5.43 (min. 0; max. 100)

Source: Snyman (forthcoming).
[a]Country in which residents were interviewed.

Table 4. Country study site comparison of percentage respondents who have had a permanent job before.

Country[a]	% who have had a permanent job before
Botswana – staff (n = 99)	21.2
Botswana – non-staff (n = 261)	21.1
Malawi – staff (n = 74)	39.2
Malawi – non-staff (n = 251)	27.1
Namibia – staff (n = 81)	40.7
Namibia – non-staff (n = 271)	18.8
South Africa – staff (n = 61)	26.2
South Africa – non-staff (n = 329)	28.6
Zambia – staff (n = 15)	73.3
Zambia – non-staff (n = 67)	25.4
Zimbabwe – staff (n = 55)	58.0
Zimbabwe – non-staff (n = 221)	28.1

Source: Snyman (2014c).
[a]Country where residents were interviewed.

was their first permanent job (Snyman, 2013), highlighting the potential importance of skills acquired through tourism for personal development and future employment opportunities.

Indirect employment is also important and results from camps using local suppliers of goods and services, camp staff attending schools and clinics in the area, camp staff spending their wages at local stores in the villages, etc. (Snyman, 2013). In Table 4, the high percentage of respondents in Zambia who had had a permanent job before is attributable to the fact that most staff interviewed had worked in the tourism camp previously when it was owned by another private sector operator and, therefore, still acquired their skills in ecotourism. Table 5 illustrates WS's workforce nationalities, showing that in the 2014–2015 reporting period, only 7% of employees were non-citizens (i.e. expatriates).

Skills training and development are provided on the job as part of the ecotourism employment package or through private sector/community business partnerships (Snyman, 2013). This can provide opportunities to develop new skills, allowing people to assume more control over their own development and to feel more confident in their abilities.

In 2015, 2558 employees were trained, of which 1210 were female and 1348 male (Wilderness Holdings, 2015). Table 6 shows the average number of hours

Table 5. Workforce nationalities (2013–2015).

Country	Citizens			Non-citizens			% Non-citizens		
	2013	2014	2015	2013	2014	2015	2013	2014	2015
Botswana	926	966	981	110	112	86	10.6	10.4	8.1
Congo	5	40	58	4	11	12	44.4	21.6	17.1
Namibia	510	536	522	10	15	8	1.9	2.7	1.5
Seychelles	84	80	92	41	40	54	32.8	33.3	37.0
South Africa	305	295	231	13	9	8	4.1	3.0	3.3
Zambia	140	121	121	8	4	2	5.4	3.2	1.6
Zimbabwe	224	226	257	4	4	4	1.8	1.7	1.5
Total	2194	2264	2262	190	195	174	8.0	7.9	7.1

Source: Wilderness Holdings (2015, p. 61).

Table 6. Average training hours per employee.

	Botswana	Congo	Namibia	Seychelles	South Africa	Zambia	Zimbabwe
2013	269	3	95	14	115	153	23
2014	326	12	55	30	54	14	18
2015	360	10	60	28	65	22	21

Source: Wilderness Holdings (2015, p. 58).

of training per employee, showing a large investment of time developing skills and building local capacity. Differences in training hours per employee between countries are attributable to various factors including staff willingness to participate in training sessions, dedicated training departments as well as the level of service required in camps, and, therefore, the level and amount of training required.

Table 7 illustrates a heavy reliance of rural households on ecotourism employment and the associated income as a means to support the household. For 59% of the staff surveyed, their salary from ecotourism was the only direct financial support for their household and for 93% of them, it constituted over 50% of the total household income (Snyman, 2014c). Namibia's lower reliance is a result of the majority of households owning cattle and using this for income, as well as the presence of government grants. In South Africa, it is lower due to a heavy reliance in the majority of interviewed households on government grants.

Table 8 further highlights the reliance on ecotourism employment as the main household income source for staff and the importance of their job to household survival.

Table 7. Staff sample only: percentage monthly household income from ecotourism.

Country[a]	100% of monthly household income from ecotourism	More than 50% of monthly household income from ecotourism
Botswana	88	94
Malawi	59	97
Namibia	42	82
South Africa	26	84
Zambia	67	100
Zimbabwe	73	100
Average	59	93

Source: Snyman (2014c).
[a]Country where residents were interviewed.

Table 8. Household income sources for staff and non-staff by location.

Country[a]	Main household income source	Second most important household income source
Botswana – staff	Job (97%)	Other[b] (2%)
Malawi – staff	Job (97.4%)	Family/Spouse (1.3%) & Weaving (1.3%)
Namibia – staff	Job (83.3%)	Other[a] (11.9%)
South Africa – staff	Job (90.3%)	Family/spouse (8.1%)
Zambia – staff	Job (100%)	N/A
Zimbabwe – staff	Job (100%)	N/A

Source: Adapted from Snyman (2013).
[a]Country where residents were interviewed.
[b]'Other' included: personal pensions, brewing beer, etc.

3.2. JVs, lease fees and other partnerships

JVs between the private sector and local communities can promote local socio-economic development through profit-sharing, employment, skills training and development as well as through the empowerment of local communities to engage in business and acquire new skills (see Snyman, 2012a, 2014b). JVs bring together the community and its natural resources, and the private sector and its business acumen, to form a partnership which can be mutually beneficial. Potential problems with JVs include divergent agendas of different parties, unclear roles and responsibilities of stakeholders, a lack of transparency and accountability, insufficient communication between stakeholders, unequal power distribution and lack of capacity in communities (Kepe, Wynberg, & Ellis, 2005). Community expectations raised to unrealistic levels by NGOs and thus negatively impacting on relationships with the private sector and ultimately on the viability of JVs are relatively common, but often undocumented.

The private sector's payment of lease fees for operating in community areas, either through JVs or lease agreements, can contribute substantially to local economic development. If lease fees are paid to a government/national institution, they can benefit local communities through investment of this income in infrastructure and development projects in the area, that is, schools and clinics. The same applies if lease fees are paid to a communal institution that could choose either to invest in a communal project, that is, borehole and water sanitation, or pay out individual/household dividends which would directly impact on household income (Snyman, 2012a). The Torra Conservancy in Namibia has successfully made use of both individual and communal benefit distribution (see Snyman, 2012a). Institutions do, however, need to be transparent and accountable for benefits to be equitably distributed in the community. There needs to be a link made between ecotourism benefits and conservation to ensure that benefits are seen to be received (Snyman, 2013). In 2013–2014, a total of USD 1.2 million in lease fees was paid by WS to various community organisations (Wilderness Holdings, 2014), and in 2014–2015 the amount was over USD 980,000 (Wilderness Holdings, 2015). Over and above the annual lease fee is payments made in terms of staff costs for these camps, including wages, food, uniform, etc. (see Table 9). In 2013–2014, a total of USD 3.1 million was paid in terms of staff and in 2014–2015, it was over USD 3.4 million (Wilderness Holdings, 2014, 2015). These values are only for the WS camps with communtiy partnerships. The company has over 50 other ecotourism camps also paying wages/salaries and the like, and, therefore, through this contributing to local socio-economic development in these areas as well. This contribution is substantial and often far exceeds lease fee payments.

3.3. Local linkages/value chains

Tourism has the potential to offer numerous local linkages that can extend its impact beyond direct employment (Meyer, 2008; Rogerson, 2012). An important part of establishing linkages is for the private sector to ascertain the skills and goods available in local communities and to develop linkages (Snyman, 2013). A common obstacle to broadening linkages around ecotourism operations is the inadequacy of skills, leaving communities unable to provide the required goods and services and being unaware of tourist demands, and therefore the types of goods and services to provide (Snyman, 2013). This problem has been widely addressed (Epler Wood International, 2004; Mitchell & Ashley, 2010; Rogerson, 2006) and the need for a multifaceted approach to promote and increase linkages stressed. To date WS has only assessed and measured local linkages in their Namibian operation (see Wilderness Holdings, 2013, 2014). Other countries where WS operates do have local linkages, but these have not yet been formally determined or measured.

3.4. Infrastructure and other socio-economic development

Infrastructural developments can have a profound impact in remote rural areas. They can be provided directly by the ecotourism operator, developed or upgraded by government specifically for ecotourism or can result from donations made by guests to philanthropic projects. Infrastructure developments, such as power, roads and communication, can have a powerful influence on people's mobility and the choices available to them, allowing them to diversify their livelihoods and reduce the risks they face (Ellis & Freeman, 2004; Mbaiwa, 2003; Snyman, 2013).

WS is involved in both community and conservation infrastructure developments. These include the development and maintenance of roads, provision of boreholes and water pumps, fitting of tracking collars on endangered species, building of schools and libraries, and fencing for community vegetable gardens (Wilderness Holdings, 2013, 2014, 2015). During the 2011–2012 financial period, WS invested or managed investments in infrastructure for public benefit across all regions to the value of more than approximately USD381,192 (Wilderness Holdings, 2012). Investments in infrastructure for public benefit were not included in later reports.

3.5. Philanthropy/donations

Table 10 shows that WS funded and/or administered more than USD 359,000 in community development and upliftment projects between March 2013 and February 2014. It was estimated by WS community development staff that these donations positively impacted the lives of approximately 13,500 people living

Table 9. WS payments made in terms of lease fees and staff costs (2013–2015).

Country	Camp	Annual value (in USD)			Staff costs (in USD)			Total value (in USD)		
		2013	2014	2015	2013	2014	2015	2013	2014	2015
Botswana	Vumbura plains, Little Vumbura	324,254	315,652	224,041	1,149,059	1,581,544	1,460,256	1,473,313	1,897,496	1,684,297
	Banoka bush camp; Khwai discover; Khwai adventurer; wilderness tented	324,254	322,753	285,253	396,569	432,338	445,977	720,823	755,090	731,231
	Moremi tented; Santawani	38,911	38,643	20,792	181,455	262,500	217,676	220,366	301,143	238,468
Congo	Ngaga, Lango	7990	35,397	54,904	150,000	155,550	273,454	157,990	190,947	328,358
Namibia	Damaraland	82,772	70,781	54,743	44,329	135,268	168,506	127,101	206,049	223,249
	Doro Nawas	51,242	62,336	52,170	48,215	144,262	180,124	99,457	206,598	232,294
	Desert Rhino; Hoanib skeleton coast	110,523	114,080	95,474	41,046	105,682	147,285	151,569	219,761	242,760
	Serra Cafema	122 005	104 570	87 516	31 486	24 213	217 740	153 491	128 784	305 255
South Africa	Pafuri Camp; Pafuri walking trails	138,695	6599	27,095	497,536	32,274	52,563	636,231	38,878	79,658
	Rocktail beach	10,191	99,448	83,719	250,997	256,367	239,185	261,187	355,815	322,904
Total		1,210,836	1,170,560	985,706	2,790,692	3,130,003	3,402,766	4,001,476	4,300,563	4,388,473

Source: Wilderness Holdings (2013, 2014, 2015).

Table 10. USD contributions to community development projects (2013–2015).

Country	2013	2014	2015	Total
Botswana	85,565	15,138	23,287	123,990
Malawi	3842	19,377	4790	28,009
Namibia	44,435	6760	12,624	63,819
South Africa	19,568	8217	4721	32,506
Zambia	857	60,362	16,288	77,507
Zimbabwe	111,146	249,862	199,225	560,233
Total	265,413	359,716	260,935	886,064

Source: Wilderness Holdings (2013, 2014, 2015).

Table 11. USD contributions to environmental education programme (2013–2015).

Country	2013	2014	2015	Total
Botswana	120,004	106,004	74,608	300,616
Limpopo Valley	35,558	63,803	9520	108,881
Malawi	53,426	38,937	53,250	145,613
Namibia	93,199	74,461	78,512	246,172
South Africa	75,310	51,854	34,460	161,624
Zambia	70,540	17,807	15,012	103,359
Zimbabwe	146,175	55,816	44,998	246,989
Total	594,213	408,681	310,360	1,313,254

Source: Wilderness Holdings (2013, 2014, 2015).

in or adjacent to PAs (Wilderness Holdings, 2014). From March 2014 to February 2015, they administered a further USD260,000 in terms of community development and upliftment projects (Wilderness Holdings, 2015). The variation in contributions between countries is largely due to the fact that WS facilitates, executes and manages some community projects on behalf of other donors, which in some areas contribute a large amount to WS projects; for example, in Zimbabwe, Grand Circle Foundation contributes to numerous community development projects with WS facilitating, implementing and managing these projects. Ecotourism can also, therefore, contribute to local socio-economic development through philanthropic donations either from the ecotourism operators themselves or from guests who visit their operation.

Table 11 shows contributions made to Children in the Wilderness (www.childreninthewilderness.com), a youth environmental education programme supported by WS: a direct contribution to local education systems and in many cases, local development. This programme only operates in areas where WS operates and is therefore directly related to the presence of private sector ecotourism in the area. Spenceley and Goodwin (2007) also found in their study in South Africa that the private sector was investing in environmental education in local communities and investing in other local socio-economic development projects.

4. Discussion

This study has shown that the private sector can impact local socio-economic development in a number of different ways including through employment, capacity building, lease fee payments, local linkages and philanthropy. Although private sector ecotourism has direct, positive impacts on local socio-economic development, employment opportunities are limited by the size of the operation and their impacts are affected by the number of different households employed. As found in this study, other authors (e.g. Ashley, 2005; Spenceley & Goodwin, 2007) have also found that the benefits of tourism are important but are generally quite specific to those employed and their families. Having a number of staff from the same family employed narrows employment benefits, and it would be useful to ensure hiring practices extend employment across as many households as possible.

Private sector partnerships with communities were shown (Table 9) to contribute substantially to local economies. It should, however, be noted that past research has shown that successful partnerships with the private sector are more likely to succeed if communities have, or establish, strong institutional structures and decision-making processes which are equitable, accountable and transparent (Snyman, 2012a, 2013, 2014b).

It was observed in this study that although private sector ecotourism is using local suppliers of goods and services, there is scope to expand this and ensure greater local impacts. In terms of growing local linkages and reducing leakages, NGOs and local governments can play an important role in training and capacity building to ensure that the level of delivery and content meet the ecotourism operators' requirements. The benefits need not be unidirectional; ecotourism operators can benefit from local linkages through reduced transport costs, improved supply logistics and fresher produce in the case of foodstuffs (Snyman, 2013). They can also improve relations with community neighbours as greater benefits from ecotourism are received. This needs to be further researched as ecotourism employment is limited by the size of the operations and it is, therefore, important to assess and analyse ways for more people to benefit and to grow ecotourism's local socio-economic impacts.

Some authors (Mazibuko, 2007; Mbaiwa, 2005) state that one of the drawbacks of ecotourism is that it employs a large percentage of expatriates and, therefore, deprives locals of employment. The data in this paper illustrated that only 7% of a total of 2346 employees were expatriates. Therefore, the company promotes employment of local people and an inflow of income, through wages paid, to local economies.

This study has shown that philanthropic donations, through the involvement of the private sector, can result in local socio-economic development that may not otherwise have occurred. As discussed by Ashley (2005), philanthropic donations can be substantial and directly targeted to current social needs, whereas business linkages generate a smaller immediate injection of cash to local communities. Business linkages can, however, be more empowering and sustainable. Ashley (2005) also highlights important business advantages to setting up linkages, including a 'social licence to operate', an enhancing of the brand, a diversification of the product for the guest, government recognition, awards, publicity, improvements in staff morale and, in some cases, cost saving (Ashley, 2005, p. 12). Future research focusing on why private sector ecotourism businesses engage in philanthropy and the related real impacts on their business would assist with understanding tourism philanthropy and the potential impacts of it on private sector businesses.

Spenceley and Goodwin (2007) also found in their study in South Africa that private sector philanthropic activities can provide a valuable source of capital investment in social utilities and services, including schools and clinics. Donations to schools, clinics, health services and various other development projects can enhance social welfare and improve local socio-economic conditions for communities. It is, however, important that donations are managed sustainably and are not administered as mere handouts (see Snyman, 2013). Overall, in WS' experience, although not without difficulties, ecotourism has proved to be instrumental in providing opportunities for local growth and development and increasing rural households' abilities to cope with the various daily challenges, especially those associated with poverty and risky environmental conditions. Difficulties have included a lack of skills and capacity in communities, unmet expectations, internal conflict within communities, or a community lacking structure or good leadership.

Further, Spenceley and Goodwin (2007, p. 255) found in their study in South Africa that isolated efforts from individual private sector tourism companies have little tangible impact on the majority of people living in highly populated rural communities, but the impacts are substantial for the few people who directly benefit. Their work highlighted the need for well-intentioned responsible tourism enterprises to consider local engagements carefully, particularly in relation to local needs and constraints (Spenceley & Goodwin, 2007). This study found similar results.

In terms of community partnerships and philanthropic donations, it is important that communities are not 'double-taxed'. This is where money from ecotourism is spent on infrastructure and services which should have been provided by government. It is also important that the private sector does not assume the role of government, fulfilling government functions in remote, rural areas, resulting in potential government complacency to invest in socio-economic development if they think that the private sector will do it instead. It is a fine line and can be difficult for the private sector to not get involved when community partners and neighbours are in need of basic goods and services.

In this paper, it has been shown that the private sector can and does contribute to local socio-economic development, directly and indirectly, through a number of different channels, including employment, business linkages, philanthropy, etc., with impacts varying according to the particular channel used.

5. Conclusion

Private sector ecotourism can certainly play an important role in terms of positive local socio-economic development through employment creation, community partnership development, facilitating and funding community projects, and providing important skills training and development. The private sector can transfer skills to local communities through in-house training programmes and mentorships, as well as sponsoring formal training courses. The development of infrastructure and improved communication, mentioned by community members interviewed in this study as an advantage of tourism development in their area, can provide opportunities for local communities to reach markets and improve livelihoods: all of which effect a positive change.

What is clear is that private sector ecotourism does effect positive change and contributes to sustainability in tourism. As discussed earlier, it is also important to take into account possible negative socio-economic developments (which were not addressed in this paper). Private sector ecotourism's long-term track record in terms of success, however, requires a future focus on ways to further engage local communities in order to further increase local socio-economic benefits and to promote long-term development. Assessment of the various ways private sector ecotourism can contribute to local development in areas of operation and beyond is important for identifying the best approach which will maximise benefits for all stakeholders. There is no one solution for all areas and the approach chosen will depend on the needs of all stakeholders, as well as their ability to engage and what they have to offer the ecotourism partnership.

Notes

1. Adapted from Snyman (2013, 2014c).
2. For more information on WS, see www.wilderness-safaris.com
3. For more details on the study sites, see Snyman (2014c, p. 5).
4. The word tourism was used in the study as that was the term most widely known in the communities. All tourism referred to in this study was ecotourism.

Acknowledgements

Special thanks also to Wilderness Safaris for accommodation, transport and logistical support.

Disclosure statement

No potential conflict of interest was reported by the author.

Funding

The author would like to gratefully acknowledge funding from the Swedish International Development Cooperation Agency (SIDA) through the Environmental Policy Research Unit (EPRU), School of Economics at the University of Cape Town.

References

Agrawal, A., & Redford, K. (2006). *Poverty, development and biodiversity conservation: Shooting in the dark?* Wildlife Conservation Society (WCS), Working Paper No. 26. Retrieved June, 29, 2010 from http://siteresources.worldbank.org/INTPOVERTYNET/Resources/Agrawal_Redford_WP26.pdf

Ahebwa, W. M., van der Duim, R., & Sandbrook, C. (2011). Tourism revenue sharing policy at Bwindi impenetrable National Park, Uganda: A policy arrangements approach. *Journal of Sustainable Tourism, 20*(3), 377–394. doi:10.1080/09669582.2011.622768

Akama, J. S., & Kieti, D. (2007). Tourism and socio-economic development in developing countries: A case study of Mombasa Resort in Kenya. *Journal of Sustainable Tourism, 15*(6), 735–748. doi:10.2167/jost543.0

Andereck, K. L., Valentine, K. M., Knopf, R. C., & Vogt, C. A. (2005). Residents' perceptions of community tourism impacts. *Annals of Tourism Research, 32*(4), 1056–1076. doi:10.1016/j.annals.2005.03.001

Armstrong, R. (2012). *An analysis of the conditions for success of community-based tourism enterprises.* International Centre for Responsible Tourism, Occassional Paper OP21. Retrieved February, 2, 2012 from http://www.artyforum.info/RTD/OP21Rebecca Armstrong.pdf

Ashley, C. (2005). *Facilitating pro-poor tourism with the private sector. Lessons learned from 'Pro-Poor Tourism Pilots in Southern Africa'.* (Working Paper No. 257). London: Overseas Development Institute. Retrieved August 25, 2010 from http://www.odi.org.uk/publications/1823-facilitating-pro-poor-tourism-private-sector-lessons-learned-pro-poor-tourism-pilots-southern-africa

Ashley, C. (2006). *How can governments boost the local economic impacts of tourism? Options and Tool.* London: Toolkit prepared for SNV and ODI. Retrieved from http://www.odi.org.uk/publications/40-can-governments-boost-local-economic-impacts-tourism

Ashley, C., Goodwin, H., & Roe, D. (2001). *Pro-poor tourism strategies: Expanding opportunities for the poor.* Pro-poor tourism briefing No. 1. Retrieved March, 23, 2011 from http://r4d.dfid.gov.uk/PDF/Outputs/Mis_SPC/R7557-Brief2.pdf

Ashley, C., & Roe, E. (2002). Making tourism work for the poor: Strategies and challenges in southern Africa. *Development Southern Africa, 19*(1), 61–82. doi:10.1080/03768350220123855

Binns, T., & Nel, E. (2002). Tourism as a local development strategy. *The Geographical Journal, 168*(3), 235–247. Retrieved May, 4, 2011 from http://www.jstor.org/stable/3451338

Blamey, R. K. (1997). Ecotourism: The search for an operational definition. *Journal of Sustainable Tourism, 5*(2), 109–130. doi:10.1080/09669589708667280

Bond, I., Child, B., de la Harpe, D., Jones, B., Barnes, J. & Anderson, H. (2004). Private land contribution to conservation in South Africa. In B. Child (Ed.), *Parks in transition* (pp 29–62). London: IUCN Earthscan.

Briedenhann, J., & Wickens, E. (2004). Tourism routes as a tool for economic development of rural areas – vibrant hope or impossible dream? *Tourism Management, 25*, 71–79. doi:10.1016/S0261-5177(03)00063-3

Ceballos-Lascuráin, H. (1996). *Tourism, ecotourism and protected areas: The state of nature-based tourism around the world and guidelines for its development.* Gland: IUCN, pp. xiv–301.

De Boer, D., van Dijk, M. P., & Tarimo, L. (2011). Business-community partnerships: The link with sustainable local tourism development in Tanzania. *Tourism and Management Studies, 7*. Retrieved March, 6, 2012 from http://tmstudies.net/index.php/ectms/article/view/336/521

De Witt, L., van der Merwe, P., & Saayman, M. (2011). *An ecotourism model for South African National Parks.* Book of proceedings Vol II – International Conference on Tourism and Management Studies, Algarve. Retrieved February, 7, 2012 from http://tmstudies.net/index.php/ectms/article/view/311

Eagles, P. F. J., McCool, S. F., & Haynes, C. D. A. (2002). *Sustainable tourism in protected areas: Guidelines for planning and management.* Switzerland : IUCN Gland, pp. xv + 183. Retrieved March, 23, 2011 from http://ecosynapsis.net/RANPAold/Contenido/MainPages/preAmac/articulosPDF/sustainable_tourism_in_pa_guidelines.pdf

Ellis, F., & Freeman, H. A. (2004). Rural livelihoods and poverty reduction strategies in 4 African countries. *The Journal of Development Studies,* 40(4), 1–30. doi:10.1080/00220380410001673175

Epler Wood International. (2004). *Evaluating ecotourism as a community and economic development strategy.* The EplerWood Report. Retrieved February, 10, 2012 from www.eplerwood.com

Fennell, D. (2008). *Ecotourism.* (3rd ed.). New York: Routledge.

Fennell, D. A. (2001). A content analysis of ecotourism definitions. *Current Issues in Tourism,* 4(5), 403–421. doi:10.1080/13683500108667896

Goodwin, H. (2008). Tourism, local economic development and poverty reduction. *Applied Research in Economic Development,* 5(3), 55–64. Retrieved from http://www.haroldgoodwin.info/uploads/ARED2008goodwin_online_v5n3_propoor_tourism.pdf

Jones, B. (2001). The evolution of a community-based approach to wildlife management at Kunene, Namibia. In D. Hulme & M. Murphree (Eds.), *African wildlife and livelihoods: The promise and performance of community conservation* (pp. 160–176). Portsmouth, NH: James Currey.

Kavita, E. & Saarinen, J. (2015). Tourism and rural community development in Namibia: Policy issues review. *Fennia* 193(3). doi:10.11143/46331

Kepe, T., Wynberg, R., & Ellis, W. (2005). Land reform and biodiversity conservation in South Africa: Complementary or in conflict? *International Journal of Biodiversity Science and Management,* 1, 3–16. doi:10.1080/17451590509618075

Mazibuko, S. (2007). Leakages and costs of ecotourism: The case of AmaZizi in the Northern Drakensberg. *Africa Insight,* 37(1), 150–168.

Mbaiwa, J. E. (2003). The socio-economic and environmental impacts of tourism development in the Okavango Delta, north-western Botswana. *Journal of Arid Environments,* 54, 447–467. doi:10.1006/jare.2002.1101

Mbaiwa, J. E. (2005). Enclave tourism and its socio-economic impacts in the Okavango Delta, Botswana. *Tourism Management,* 26(2), 157–172. doi:10.1016/j.tourman.2003.11.005

Meyer, D. (2008). Pro-poor tourism: From leakages to linkages. A conceptual framework for creating linkages between the accommodation sector and 'poor' neighbouring communities. *Current Issues in Tourism,* 10, 558–583. doi:10.2167/cit313.0

Mitchell, J., & Ashley, C. (2010). *Tourism and poverty reduction: Pathways to prosperity.* London: Earthscan publications.

Novelli, M., & Scarth, A. (2007). Tourism in protected areas: Integrating conservation and community development in Liwonde National Park, Malawi. *Tourism and Hospitality Planning and Development,* 4(1), 47–73. doi:10.1080/14790530701289697

Rogerson, C. M. (2006). Pro-poor local economic development in South Africa: The role of pro-poor tourism. *Local Environment,* 11(1), 37–60. doi:10.1080/13549830500396149

Rogerson, C. M. (2012). Tourism-agriculture linkages in rural South Africa: Evidence from the accommodation sector. *Journal of Sustainable Tourism,* 20(3), 477–496. doi:10.1080/09669582.2011.617825

Sandbrook, C. G. (2010). Putting leakage in its place: The significance of retained tourism revenue in the local context in rural Uganda. *Journal of International Development, 22*, 124–136. doi:10.1002/jid.1507

Simpson, M. (2008). The impacts of tourism initiatives on rural livelihoods and poverty reduction. In A. Spenceley (Ed.), *Responsible Tourism: Critical issues for conservation and development* (pp. 239–266). London: Earthscan, IUCN.

Snyman, S. (2012a). Ecotourism joint ventures between the private sector and communities: An updated analysis of the Torra Conservancy and Damaraland Camp partnership, Namibia. *Tourism Management Perspectives, 4*, 127–135. doi:10.1016/j.tmp.2012.07.004

Snyman, S. (2012b). The role of ecotourism employment in poverty reduction and community perceptions of conservation and tourism in southern Africa. *Journal of Sustainable Tourism, 20*(3), 395–416. doi:10.1080/09669582.2012.657202

Snyman, S. (2013). *High-end ecotourism and rural communities in southern Africa: A socio-economic analysis* (Doctoral thesis), School of Economics, Faculty of Commerce, University of Cape Town.

Snyman, S. (2014b). Partnership between a private sector ecotourism operator and a local community in the Okavango Delta, Botswana: The case of the Okavango Community Trust and Wilderness Safaris. *Journal of Ecotourism.* doi:10.1080/14724049.2014.980744

Snyman, S. (2014c). The impact of ecotourism employment on rural household incomes and social welfare in six southern African countries. *Tourism and Hospitality Research, 14*(1–2), 37–52. doi:10.1177/1467358414529435

Snyman, S. (forthcoming). *Where does the ecotourism dollar go? A southern African perspective.* Under review.

Spenceley, A. (2003). *Tourism, local livelihoods, and the private sector in South Africa: Case studies on the growing role of the private sector in natural resource management.* Sustainable Livelihoods in Southern Africa Research Paper 8, Institute of Development Studies, Brighton. Retrieved September, 1, 2010 from http://r4d.dfid.gov.uk/PDF/Outputs/Livelihoodsresearch/wRP08.pdf

Spenceley, A., & Goodwin, H. (2007). Nature-based tourism and poverty alleviation: Impacts of private sector and parastatal enterprises in and around Kruger National Park, South Africa. *Current Issues in Tourism, 10*(2&3), 255–277. doi:10.2167/cit305.0

Stronza, A., & Pêgas, F. (2008). Ecotourism and conservation: Two cases from Brazil and Peru. *Human Dimensions of Wildlife, 13*, 263–279. doi:10.1080/10871200802187097

Stronza, A. L. (2010). Commons management and ecotourism: Ethnographic evidence from the Amazon. *International Journal of the Commons, 4*(1), 56–77.

Telfer, D. J., & Sharpley, R. (2008). *Tourism and development in the developing world.* London: Routledge.

Varghese, G. (2008). Public-private partnerships in South African National Parks: The rationale, benefits and lessons learned. In Spenceley, A. (Ed.), *Responsible tourism: Critical issues for conservation and development* (pp. 69–84). London: Earthscan.

Vedeld, P., Jumane, A., Wapalila, G., & Songorwa, A. (2012). Protected areas, poverty and conflicts: A livelihoods case study of Mikumi National Park, Tanzania. *Forest Policy and Economics, 21*, 20–31. doi:10.1016/j.forpol.2012.01.008

Wilderness Holdings. (2012). *Wilderness integrated annual report 2012.* Retrieved April 19, 2012 from http://www.wildernessgroup.com/system/assets/125/original/2012%20Community.pdf?1343722079

Wilderness Holdings. (2013). *Wilderness integrated annual report 2013.* Retrieved September 20, 2015 from http://www.wilderness-group.com/system/assets/142/original/Wilderness%20IR%202013%20-%20Web.pdf?1375184197

Wilderness Holdings. (2014). *Wilderness integrated annual report 2014.* Retrieved September 20, 2015 from http://www.wilderness-group.com/system/assets/149/original/Wilderness_IAR_2014_WEB.pdf?1407143997

Wilderness Holdings. (2015). *Wilderness integrated annual report 2015.* Retrieved August 1, 2015 from http://www.wilderness-group.com/system/assets/165/original/Integrated_Annual_Report_2015_(full_Report).pdf?1438585754

A new model for guide training and transformative outcomes: a case study in sustainable marine-wildlife ecotourism

Kaye Walker and Betty Weiler

ABSTRACT

Interactive experiences with non-captive, charismatic, marine megafauna, such as whales and dolphins, present a growing ecotourism trend with potentially positive and negative sustainability outcomes. Its sustainable future in countries recently developing this type of tourism is dependent upon not only operational best practices and management, but also the extent to which such experiences contribute to positive change to pro-environmental awareness, attitudes and behaviours of both local guides and tourists. This paper presents a new guide training model that was developed from empirical research and has been utilised to train local guides in Tonga. The Guiding Model links tourists' intentional post-experience behaviours with the guiding and interpretive elements of ecotourism activities using means-end analysis and a ladder of abstraction questioning process called the PIIA. The paper outlines the use of the model to develop the first nationally accredited swim-with-whale guide training programme in the South Pacific. Application of the training model is described and examined with respect to its capacity to underpin positive sustainability effects in the broader sense and upon tourists' pro-environmental perceptions through the facilitation of the local guides' awareness, reflection and appreciation of their role in achieving contemporary ecotourism goals, and linking these to their personal values.

Introduction and case study background

Ecotourism, of which wildlife ecotourism can be regarded as a subset, has maintained significant global growth (Ballantyne & Packer, 2013), with a particular component of the market emerging: the interactive, non-captive, marine wildlife experience (Cater & Cater, 2007; Lück, 2008). Not content with watching from boats, tourists now wish to swim in the open ocean and to interact with charismatic mega-fauna (Curtin, 2005) such as sharks (Dobson, 2008) and ever more so, dolphins and whales (Constantine & Bejder, 2008). Over 56 types of marine mammals, representing 43% of their known species, have now become the focus of in-situ tourism activities in 120 countries (Walker & Hawkins, 2013). The whale ecotourism industry alone demonstrated a remarkable 14% growth rate in the South Pacific from 1998 to 2008 (Walker & Hawkins, 2013). Many of these marine wildlife experiences are in developing nations, or at least nations just developing this type of tourism, transitioning or enhancing the use of their ocean resources from catching and eating marine animals, to using them to create an ecotourism industry (Cunningham, Huijbens, & Wearing, 2012). As a result, there is often minimal related local management experience or expertise among the host community, or even access to training in this type of tourism.

It has been suggested that wildlife tourism's increasing popularity is due to greater ease of access to wildlife destinations and increased public interest and awareness of environmental issues (Ballantyne, Packer, & Falk, 2011; Higginbottom, 2004; Newsome, Dowling, & Moore, 2004; Rodger, Moore, & Newsome, 2007). This literature notes the potential benefits for environmental sustainability and local conservation by capitalising on this growing awareness with informed and managed experiential ecotourism as a purportedly though sometimes disputed non-consumptive activity (Buckley, 2013; Higginbottom, 2004). The sustainable future of these wildlife ecotourism operations (i.e. wildlife tourism underpinned by ecotourism principles which, for simplicity, we henceforth refer to as wildlife tourism), stakeholder communities, and the marine animals and their habitats depend not only on responsible management and operational best practices *in situ*, but also the extent to which the experience facilitates positive environmental perspectives, fostering longer-term pro-environmental attitudes and behaviours among both host populations and tourists (Packer & Ballantyne, 2013).

Accordingly, the primary aim of this paper is to introduce a training approach for ecotourism guides that empower them to respond to the contemporary goals of ecotourism and effect positive change among tourists and among the guides themselves. In this paper, we use the term whale guide, wildlife guide and ecotourism guide interchangeably and, following Black and Weiler (2013), define an ecotourism guide as someone who is employed on a paid or voluntary basis and conducts paying or non- paying visitors around natural (but may include cultural) attractions, areas or sites, utilising ecotourism and interpretation principles. In other words, she or he communicates and interprets the significance of the environment, promotes minimal impact practices and advances the sustainability of the natural and cultural environment. The paper presents a specific Guiding Model developed from empirical research, and an associated interpretive process designed to facilitate such a transformative experience called the Personal Insight Interpretive Approach (or PIIA). The secondary aim of the paper is to critically describe the application of the model to a training programme for guides who facilitate interactive marine wildlife experiences. The effectiveness of this training and the Guiding Model in positively impacting the guides, ensuring ecotourism principles are perceived as integral to their guiding role, and hence underpinning longer-term positive outcomes regarding the tourists, the industry, the species and broader sustainability perspectives is examined.

In the context of interactive experiences with non-captive wildlife such as whales, effecting positive change centres on the local tour guides employed to manage the swim-with-whale experience. However, local guides in developing countries can have quite different socio-cultural and socio-environmental ideologies to that of a Western-orientated ecotourism philosophy, and may lack the underpinning environmental perspectives more commonly found among those trained as tour guides in developed countries, and thus normally associated with guiding in a sustainable manner. It is also unlikely they will have experienced training that promotes pro-environmental attitudes and behaviours that can underpin conservation of marine species, many of which are migratory or nomadic (Walker & Hawkins, 2013). This is specifically relevant for the focus of the case study presented here: the International Union for Conservation of Nature-listed endangered South Pacific Humpback whales who travel thousands of kilometres between summer feeding locations and sheltered winter breeding and birthing sites. In the process this endangered population crosses numerous international boundaries experiencing differing socio-cultural and environmental values, policies and politics (Walker & Moscardo, 2011), ranging from whale hunting, to watching, to swimming with them in Tonga, one of the few places in the world that endorses this activity in a critical birthing and breeding location (IFAW, 2009).

The case study presented involves the development and delivery of the Tonga Whale Guide Training Program (TWGTP), which is the first nationally accredited swim-with-whale guide training programme in the South Pacific region, and possibly the first globally. The training programme was developed and made mandatory for all industry guides in response to Tonga's aim to facilitate sustainable management and best practices for their rapidly growing and major national tourism industry involving swimming with Humpback whales (Kessler & Harcourt, 2010). The Tonga government and industry representative organisations also hoped to address noted issues regarding the local guides' resistance to follow sustainable practices and guidelines, and the consequent international scrutiny and controversy regarding the operations of this industry (Walker & Moscardo, 2011). The sustainability of this whale population is inherently linked to the suckling of the calves in these sheltered waters, uninterrupted by tourists, boating or other commercial activities in order to enable adequate growth and energy for their successful migration to polar locations only months after their birth.

Literature review

Ecotourism, sustainability, guiding and interpretation

Ecotourism has often sought to effect positive change at the local level, particularly with respect to conservation outcomes (Ceballos-Lascurin, 1996; Honey, 1999; Mowforth & Munt, 1998; Ross & Wall, 2001; Smith, 2001; Wearing & Neil, 1999; Weaver, 2001). In addition, ecotourism activities have been expected to include an educational component, implemented via interpretation which aims to increase tourist knowledge and awareness and manage the impacts of their behaviours on site (Ballantyne & Uzzel, 1999; Ham & Weiler, 2002; McArthur & Hall, 1996; Moscardo & Ballantyne, 2008). The literature has since described ecotourism's sustainability goals more broadly to include the socio-environmental aspects in particular, such as personal responsibility for sustainability issues and actions and developing an ethic of care (Jamal & Camargo, 2014; Mair & Laing, 2013; Miller, Rathouse, Scarles, Holmes, & Tribe, 2010). The International Ecotourism Society (TIES) most recently defines ecotourism as: 'responsible travel to natural areas that conserves the environment, sustains the well-being of the local people, and involves interpretation and education' (TIES, 2015). TIES (2015) note that '*education* is meant to be inclusive of both staff and guests' and that the principles include building 'environmental and cultural awareness and respect' and the delivery of 'memorable interpretive experiences to visitors that help raise sensitivity to host countries' political, environmental, and social climates'. Interpretation has been defined by Interpretation Australia (2011) to include the socio-environmental aspect as 'a means of communicating ideas and feelings which help people understand more about themselves and their environment', and is often described as a critical element in ecotourism (Tsang, Yeung, & Cheung, 2011).

Employing local guides has been identified as a key mechanism to enhancing positive outcomes for both local conservation and for tourists and their experience (Moscardo, Woods, & Saltzer, 2004). Guides are increasingly called upon to move beyond the narrowly focused 'educational' goal of interpretation in ecotourism (Ablett & Dyer, 2009) to being able to assist tourists to identify their personal role and responsibility in sustainability outcomes. Impacting visitor attitudes and behaviours beyond the specific tourist experience (Ballantyne, Packer, & Falk, 2011; Packer & Ballantyne, 2013) and other contemporary expectations of guides are consistent with Tilden's (1977) set of core principles for effective interpretive practices which suggest the facilitation of deeply personal, insightful and transformative outcomes. The essence of this is described by Walker and Moscardo (2014) as: 'connecting the interpretive experience to the visitor's personal life and addressing their individuality; seeking to provoke or stimulate a response or revelation in the visitor rather than merely presenting information; and offering interpretation as a holistic experience' (p. 1176).

The critical role of the guide in fostering sustainable wildlife tourism is well established in the literature (Ballantyne, Packer, & Hughes, 2009; Curtin, 2010; Moscardo, 2013; Moscardo et al., 2004; Weiler & Black, 2015; Weiler & Ham, 2001). There has also been recent research specifically dedicated to addressing and understanding tourists' subsequent sustainable behaviours and attitudes as a result of their ecotourism and interpretive experiences (Ballantyne & Packer, 2011; Kerstetter, Jou, & Lin, 2004; Kim, Airey, & Szivas, 2011; Packer & Ballantyne, 2013). Such desired outcomes present a greater challenge for the ecotourism guide than merely providing information and direction for the tourist, arguably requiring considerable deliberation in the design, delivery and evaluation of interpretive practices and outcomes, and in the training of those employed to facilitate these outcomes.

Ecotourism guide training

Weiler and Black (2015) acknowledge there are many very good training materials and products including texts, workbooks and video packages which include effective communication and interpretation techniques (e.g. Ballantyne, Weiler, Crabtree, Ham, & Hughes, 2000; Pastorelli, 2003). However, Christie and Mason (2003) who reviewed guide training programmes and organisations in Australia, New Zealand, Canada, the United States of America; and the United Kingdom, along with Weiler and Black (2015), note that many training programmes are limited to the achievement of competency-based benchmarks. Furthermore, training for ecotourism guides in developing countries including the South Pacific is often based on Western-orientated programmes established by wildlife conservation NGOs or Australian technical colleges, modified for delivery by private consultants who tend not to incorporate recent theoretical constructs or empirical findings (Black & King, 2002; Weiler & Ham, 2002). Hence, it has been suggested these programmes can fall short of adequately equipping guides to meet desired ecotourism outcomes (Black & Weiler, 2013; Kohl, 2007; Weiler & Black, 2015).

More recent guiding research is exploring the interpretive and experiential processes involved in facilitating 'transformative' tourist outcomes, regarded as those that increase awareness and create long-lasting impacts through powerful affective, cognitive and behavioural responses (Ballantyne, Packer, & Sutherland, 2011; Christie & Mason, 2003; Weaver & Lawton, 2007). Christie and Mason (2003) argued that for guides to be effective experience-brokers as well as to effect change, they need to be trained to be more critically reflective practitioners. They propose a training model orientated towards 'transforming' the guide and suggest the use of training techniques to facilitate recognition, confrontation and reflection of trainees' own assumptions, values, tour aims and objectives. Unfortunately, Christie and Mason (2003) do not provide any specific techniques to achieve this transformative process, however, relevant findings and recommendations in Weiler and Black (2015) that resonate with the training approach presented in this paper involve: the host country identifying, driving and owning the training programme (Weiler & Ham, 2002); a culturally sensitive approach (Weiler & Ham, 2002); and consideration of the local guides' perceptions of their roles (Ballantyne & Hughes, 2001); in order to develop a more flexible, co-created, experience-focused and critically reflective approach to training and delivery (Christie & Mason, 2003; Kohl, Brown, & Humke, 2001).

The development of the guiding model, PIIA and training approach

The guide training approach used in theTWGTP was informed by a review of contemporary ecotourism and guide training literature as summarised here regarding interpretation principles and personal development through reflective processes. The Guiding Model presented is an outcome of empirical research which aimed to specifically identify and link the elements of the ecotourism experience and associated interpretation with tourists' experiential outcomes and intentional post-experience sustainable behaviours (see Walker & Moscardo, 2014). The research methodology involved an adaptation of the means-end analytical approach (Klenosky, Frauman, Norman, & Gengler, 1998) using a survey to encourage participants to deeply reflect on their ecotourism experience and outcomes. Means-end analysis is considered to offer 'a potentially valuable framework to understand pro-environmental and pro-social behaviour in terms of underlying personal values' (Jägel, Keeling, Reppel, & Gruber, 2012, p. 376). It does this via a sequence of open-ended questions that help participants to identify and link the experiential attributes with perceived benefits and personal values and insights (a cognitive process referred to as laddering, or the ladder of abstraction approach), from which attribute–benefit–value (ABV) chains can be constructed for each respondent. A subsequent prompting question linking these to the respondent's intentional post-experience behaviours finalises this process. Personally significant values are considered to drive an individual's behaviours, and the chains for all respondents are combined and summarised in a Hierarchical Value Map (HVM) which graphically illustrates the relationships between all these elements via the linkages in a tiered ABV format (Jägel et al., 2012) leading to behavioural intentions. The combination of these factors resulted in the development of an adapted HVM which was then referred to as the Value Model of Interpretation (Walker & Moscardo, 2014). Specific details of the empirical investigation including approach, field design, data collection and analysis involving 349 participants of marine-based, multi-activity, 12-day ecotourism tours in three case studies are outlined in Walker (2007).

The Guiding Model as presented in Figure 1 consists of a pyramid that graphically represents the HVM tiered construction (referred to above as the Value Model of Interpretation), but in a simpler format consisting of levels (base to pinnacle) for application in theTWGTP. It presents the attributes (in the 1st level, Level 1) that must be initially facilitated to stimulate benefits (Level 2), and subsequent value identification (Level 3) and personal insights (Level 4) which may stimulate corresponding behaviours that are environmentally positive (the pinnacle outcome) (i.e. this model does not include the myriad linkages of interpretive and experiential pathways possible between each element which appear in the HVM). This formed the theoretical and practical premise of the training programme, including how and when to incorporate the elements presented in the model into the guides interpretation and ecotourism activities. For example, the foundation Level 1 'attributes' can be addressed via training that develops guides' expertise, knowledge, skill and dedication in establishing a safe, secure and trusting environment for engaging tourists in activities that may be outside their usual comfort zone. The establishment of these attributes in practice facilitate Level 2 benefits, allowing tourists to not only safely and enjoyably immerse themselves in the experience, but also enhances their receptiveness to environmental messages and thus overall environmental awareness.

Guides are trained to use interpretation to move tourists upward through this pyramid, linking benefits to personal values and perceptions by encouraging

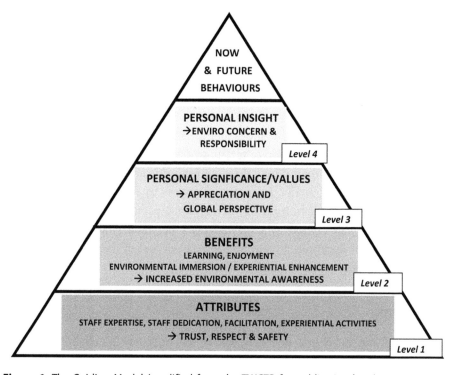

Figure 1. The Guiding Model (modified from the TWGTP for publication here).

them to reflect more deeply upon the experience, its personal significance and its potential impact on subsequent environmental behaviours. The interpretive practice designed to help guides facilitate tourists' engagement in this cognitive process has been called the Personal Insight Interpretive Approach, or PIIA, to encourage the guide to 'peer' into the tourists' minds. It involves asking tourists a series of simple questions to initially identify the 'best' things about the ecotourism experience and what makes these the best thing, effectively eliciting attributes (Level 1) and perceived benefits (Level 2). This discussion is followed by queries as to why or in what way these are personally important to encourage the deeper consideration and reflection of personal values (Level 3) and insights (Level 4), identified in the model as being feelings of appreciation, global perspectives, environmental responsibility, care or concern. Group interaction and the dynamic exchange of ideas within an ecotourism experience often helps this process in making participants more aware of others' perceived 'best' things, benefits or personal significance, which contributes to the co-creation of the experiential outcomes and can help facilitate the guide's concluding and more provocative, transformative question in this sequence, that is 'whether they are inspired to adopt any particular environmental actions or behaviours, or make any changes in their lives as a consequence of this experience'. The PIIA and its series of questions as described, effectively mimics the Means-end laddering sequence of questions used in the original empirical research to facilitate participants' cognitive responses in their identification and relation of attributes, benefits, values and subsequent intentional behaviours (Walker & Moscardo, 2014), and that stimulated the subsequent development of the Guiding Model.

The Means-end question approach was also used as a teaching aid in the TWGTP to encourage the trainee guides' own reflection of the training programme and its goals to facilitate their own personal insights and connections to their ecotourism role, and thus subsequent intentional, and hopefully environmentally sustainable actions in their ecotours. It was incorporated into reflective exercises to help the trainee guides identify the attributes, perceived benefits and importance they placed upon different aspects of their job, their role and the role of ecotourism in their lives, their community and their region locally, nationally and internationally. It engaged trainees to work through a process of appraising their own assumptions, perceptions, personal characteristics and values, and how this related to achieving their personal goals in their career, life or within their community, and importantly as part of their role in facilitating these types of ecotourism experiences.

The TWGTP

The TWGTP was developed and delivered by the authors (in collaboration with others) in 2012 to train guides who lead groups of overseas tourists to swim with Humpback whales in the wild in Tongan waters. It was informed by best practice ecotourism and interpretation principles, and the theory and empirical findings as discussed. The many considerations and range of stakeholders and communication involved in developing the programme are not all addressed here, but are in the final partner report (Walker, Weiler, & Cvetko, 2012), while other interpretive training tools and outcomes are currently described in Weiler and Walker (2014). Rather, this paper focuses on the evaluative and qualitative outcomes of the training programme with respect to the use of the Guiding Model, the PIIA and the reflective Means-end teaching approach described above. These components of the TWGTP were integrated with associated training materials and topics which included: a general introduction involving local, regional and global perspectives of tourism and marine wildlife tourism; understanding tourists, their expectations and experience; and ecotourism guiding goals addressing contemporary sustainability perspectives in relation to the Guiding model and the PIIA.

The additional topics addressed by the four-person team (plus two Tongan language interpreters and assistants) over the five days of training included: tour planning; interpretive guiding practices; group management; Humpback whale information; industry regulations; risk management and operational skills. The delivery included lectures, group discussions, activities and role-playing sessions (both in and out of the classroom), demonstrations, and reflective exercises to identify and link the training material with personal development, significance and values.

It is pertinent to the findings to identify the characteristics of the training participants who are the respondents in this study. They represented all the current Swim with Humpback whale tourism operators in Tonga and a substantial proportion of their staff (whale guides and other workers such as skippers, crew, office staff or managers) who worked for these operators at the time. A questionnaire was sent to all potential training participants prior to the programme commencing. Responses from 65 of the final 68 training participants were returned. Most of this sample consisted of local Tongans (74%) and the rest being expatriate owner-operators or guides. In response to a question regarding skills they currently held and felt would help most in the training programme and becoming a whale guide, 70% identified only their ability to swim and speak English, along with relaxed and friendly attitudes. Two-thirds of the sample stated they had no previous guiding experience, with this group consisting largely of fishermen, skippers and crew. Thus, there was not only limited previous guiding experience particularly within the Tongan complement, there was even less exposure revealed with regard to ecotourism principles or philosophy as many of those with guiding experience did not have a background of any formal guide training. Guides in this industry often progressed from employment as a deck-hand, for example, because they can swim or speak an acceptable level of English, not because of their qualifications in ecotourism or guiding, nor their environmental ethics or attitudes. All of these factors are likely to have contributed to the significant impact and perceived effectiveness of the training programme, particularly with regard to the Tongan complement. In contrast, many of the 26% expatriate complement described themselves as having substantial experience or adequate training in ecotourism guiding prior to the TWGTP delivery, yet the statistics reported in the results section suggest they were also positively impacted by the training.

Methods

Pre- and post-training surveys were provided to all 68 training participants to complete on a voluntary basis at the beginning and immediately following the training programme (Kirkpatrick, 1983). These were administered using a respondent numbering system that preserved the anonymity of the participant to reduce social desirability bias, while allowing for matched-pairs analysis. Both closed self-rating scale questions and open-ended questions were included. The pre- and post-training surveys included an identical set of 30 questions regarding skills, knowledge and awareness associated with the training programme and material. The participants answered each of the questions from two perspectives: (i) how *well they could perform* these skills or *had this knowledge*; and (ii) *how important* they felt these skills or knowledge were to their guiding role. Respondents rated themselves on a scale from 1 to 5, from 'I can't do this or I don't know this' (1) to 'I can do this really well or I know this really well' (5), and from 'Not important' (1) to 'Essential' (5), respectively.

The responses presented here include only those that are relevant to the focus of this paper, that is, topics regarding ecotourism, tourists and the role of guiding (11 questions in total). The questions asked about: the guide's role and goals in ecotourism, and its place in Tonga; the Guiding Model and their guiding approach; tourist types, motivations and expectations; and how their guiding role may link to their personal goals and values. Open-ended questions in the post-training survey sought the respondents' deeper reflection regarding the importance and personal significance of the programme and this sort of tourism. This section included an abbreviated laddering sequence from the means-end approach (Jägel et al., 2012; Klenosky et al., 1998), as adapted for the PIIA and as previously described.

The sample size (*n*) for the results reported here varied between 44 and 49. The statistical analysis used for the identical scale questions was a paired-sample *t*-test to determine if there was a significant difference between each respondent's pre- and post-training responses ($p < .05$). The open-ended questions were qualitatively analysed using the SPSS Text Analytics software designed to identify recurring themes and concepts in relatively short answer responses. These respondent-derived categories and their response examples were subsequently analysed by a second coder familiar with the results and questionnaire and then independently considered by a third coder who was an experienced researcher and trainer in the programme. The final categories for these open-ended responses represent a consensus between the three coders and are presented in the second section of the results.

Results

(1) Pre- and post-training survey: understanding ecotourism, tourists and the role of guiding

Figure 2 presents the pre- and post-training means for the 11 closed self-rated questions. The questions were worded to be consistent with the content of the training programme but appear in a summarised form in Figure 2. The mean ratings of post-training *knowledge* were found to be significantly higher (p < .05). All mean ratings of perceived *importance* were also significantly higher post-training, except for Questions about: describing the differences between wildlife tourists and other types of tourists (a); and describing their goals for guiding and what they want to achieve in the tours (f). This may be due to the high rating of importance already ascribed to these items in the pre-training questionnaire (4.40 and 4.43, respectively), and hence were unlikely to be significantly different post-training. It is perhaps pertinent though that describing their guiding goals (f) had the highest rating of importance and the second highest rating of knowledge post-training. This point is revisited in the analysis of the open-ended questions in the section '(2) Participant responses about personally important training outcomes'.

There are two survey components presenting particularly notable increases in participant knowledge development. The first component involved three items relating to the 'essential guide attributes as described in the Guiding Model', 'the steps (or levels) in the Guiding Model' and 'the participants' guiding approach' (Questions e, g and h, respectively, representing increases of 1.04, 1.18 and 0.96). The second component involves notable increases in two items relating to 'how their guiding role helps achieve their personal goals or ambitions' and 'how their guiding role relates to their personal, community or cultural values' (Questions j and k which, respectively, presented increases in knowledge of 1.00 and 1.04). The significance of these responses is enhanced by noting the question recording the highest rating of post-training knowledge, that is about being able to explain what whale tourism means for Tonga (Question c), and upon which they elaborated in their open-ended question responses (see the section '(2) Participant responses about personally important training outcomes').

(2) Participant responses about personally important training outcomes

The following tables present participant response categories (descriptions and examples) to the open-ended questions about the most important things they

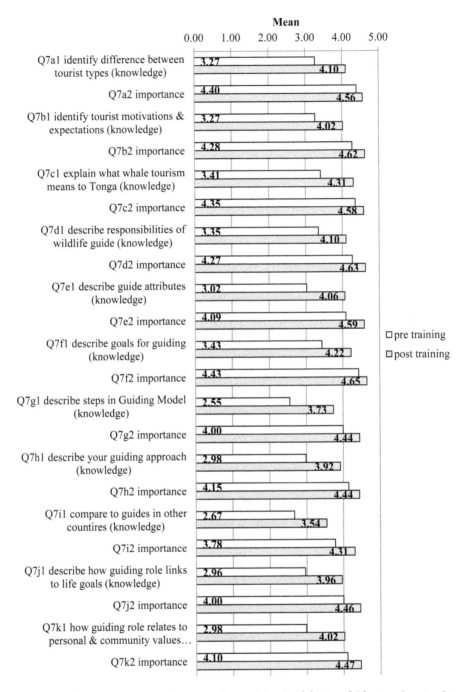

Figure 2. Guide responses to questions regarding training Modules 1 and 5 (ecotourism, tourists, guiding roles and the Guiding Model).

learned or took away from the training programme regarding 'this sort of tourism' (Table 1) and 'anything else that is important to them personally' (Table 2). These responses complement the previous results by providing the participants' more descriptive reflections and personal insights in relation to the self-rating responses about the principles, management and importance of ecotourism and their guiding role.

Table 1 indicates the majority of responses focused on insights regarding tourist management (as per the first two self-rating questions). It was evident during the programme delivery and exercises the guides had little knowledge about tourist typology or expectation management (as per the first two response examples in Category 1.1). Hence, it is revealing with regard to the training outcomes that the participants went from such little consideration of the tourist experience to identifying how it *can have an impact on how tourists think about the environment of a whale* (third response in Category 1.1). There was also concern expressed for managing the tourists' *high expectations* (Category 1.1 and 1.4). Numerous respondents acknowledged how *unique* this ecotourism experience was (i.e. swimming with Humpback whale mothers and newborn calves), its *fragility* and how significant this industry is for Tonga, and hence the importance to conduct their roles *properly*, as emphasised in responses to Categories 1.2 through to 1.5, for example:

> Whale swimming is unique and can be Tonga's number 1 revenue if looked after. (1.2)
> Doing our job as a guide properly so the industry becomes more and more economic. (1.3)

Table 1. Important training outcomes about this type of ecotourism.

Category	Description and examples	No. of responses	% of responses
1.1 Tourist Interactions & Outcomes	**Insights regarding tourist management and experiential outcomes.** *Expectations are high and need to be managed properly. Tourists are all very different and there are different ways to approach them. That it can have an impact on how tourists think about the environment of a whale.*	22	45
1.2 Tonga's Whale Ecotourism Industry	**Insights regarding the industry and its operations.** *Whale swimming is unique and can be Tonga's number 1 revenue if looked after. A fragile industry which could easily change to pressures of whaling. Very competitive. Needs collaboration and better accommodation.*	12	24.4
1.3 Role of Guiding	**Identification of guiding role in relation to industry and tourists.** *Doing our job as a guide properly so the industry becomes more and more economic. Tourists must have to obey the role of the guide and need their attention when the guide talks.*	5	10.2
1.4 Whale Tour	**Significance of this type of tour and objectives.** *Whale swimming is unique to other guided tours, but can we manage expectations of tourists. Making the tour more enjoyable.*	5	10.2
1.5 Whales	**Whale conservation and knowledge.** *Importance to do properly for both the whale future as well as Tonga tourism. I can know more about the whale.*	5	10.2
Total		49	100

Table 2. Important training outcomes of personal significance.

Category	Description and examples	No. of responses	% of responses
2.1 Tonga & Industry	**Linking of industry with Tonga and sustainability issues.** *This particular water-based activity is vital for tourism in the whale kingdom of Tonga.* *To help improve standard and understanding to environment. Environmental issues of pollution and interaction to be discussed with other skippers.*	19	29
2.2 Guiding & Future	**Guiding role associated with the future personally.** *This is a great programme for local guides and hopefully they can see this and recognise the opportunity to educate themselves more.* *Looking forward to further study for better job opportunities.* *To be a good guide I need to use more knowledge and be more professional.*	14	21.5
2.3 ID of Personal Goals	**Identification of personal goals associated with guiding role.** *Yes, my goal is guiding and to provide our community with awareness programme on whales and environment would be life rewarding experience.* *Yes, my goal is to show people (guests) how important the humpback whale is in our society.*	13	20
2.4 Environmental Awareness	**Environmental awareness and understanding on a regional, national or global level.** *I am to be a professional guide and be able to help other locals to develop their knowledge about our marine life and how important they are to us.* *For people to get more involved and engaged in safeguarding whales.*	12	18.5
2.5. World Perspective	**Tonga's relationship with the rest of the world.** *Whale – they unite Tonga with the rest of the world.* *The world – we care about the world, the world cares about us.*	4	6
2.6 Tourist Interactions & Outcomes	**The benefit of interactions with regard to conveying societal values and contributing to national sustainability.** *One important thing is improve my skills for guiding as I know it helps to attract the tourists.* *Show tourists how important the humpback whale is to us.*	3	5
Total		65	100

These categories all linked to the importance of the industry to Tonga and consequently its careful management and conduct, which addresses one of the primary aims of this training programme as noted in the introduction – to inspire best practice among the local guides.

Table 2 reports participants' perceptions of what was personally significant about the training. Category 2.1 seems to be an extension of the responses previously discussed, in particular the importance of this industry to Tonga. However, broader sustainability issues and perceived benefits also emerged, such as the need to improve the industry *standard* and address issues of *pollution* and boat *interaction* with the whales. Categories 2.2, 2.3 and 2.4 were more revealing with regard to participants' personal significance and goals and collectively present 46 responses, the largest component proportion across the two tables. These sample responses elaborate on the higher scale self-rated responses discussed in the section '(1) Pre- and post-training survey' and indicate personal reflection and linkages particularly with sustainability issues in their own community, as well as personally and with regard to the industry:

To be a good guide I need to use more knowledge and be more professional.

Yes, my goal is guiding and to provide our community with awareness program on whales and environment would be life rewarding experience.

I am to be a professional guide and be able to help other locals to develop their knowledge about our marine life and how important they are to us.

Finally, there was some recognition of the importance of the whales and this type of tourism on a more global perspective in Categories 2.5 and 2.6, suggesting the whales *unite Tonga with the rest of the world*, and participants' desire to *show tourists how important the humpback whale is to us*. While there were only a few of these responses they suggest a substantial change in the local guide perspectives as a result of the training.

Discussion and future research

Both the quantitative and qualitative results provide some powerful illustrations of positive change as an outcome of the training, and as a consequence, potential impacts on tourists as well. The results of the self-rated pre- and post-training questions indicate significant positive changes in perceptions of importance of the elements of the Guiding Model with regard to the participants' guiding role and responsibilities, and thus suggest that one of the aims of the training programme appears to have been achieved: to ensure ecotourism principles are viewed as integral to the guides' role, and to enhance appreciation of the inherent role of the tourists and tourist management in achieving sustainability goals.

It is acknowledged that this type of in-class post-training evaluation can be biased for a number of reasons, including participants' motivations and interpretation of the intent of the evaluation. However, responses to the open-ended questions reinforce and extend reported perceptions via the self-rating questions regarding the training outcomes. These emphasise the guides' perceived role regarding management of the tourists and increasing their environmental awareness, along with other insights about the industry, its operations and significance to Tonga. The responses also describe the links made between their guiding role and their personal goals, environmental sustainability and their communities.

While the open-ended responses cannot conclude or attribute that actual positive 'change' occurred as a result of the training, the sample information collected prior to training regarding the participants' previous experience and perceptions of guiding and their current skills, along with the research findings, do suggest considerable critical reflection on the part of the guides regarding their own values and perceptions and the role they play in the ecotourism industry. As per the aim of the Guiding Model and use of the PIIA to enhance the guides' capacity to facilitate 'transformative' experiences by interacting with and influencing the tourists' experiential perceptions, values and post-experience actions, it was suggested in the literature review that guide training programmes should develop the guide's own ability to be a critically reflective and flexible practitioner with the skills to co-create the ecotourism experience (Ballantyne & Hughes, 2001; Christie & Mason, 2003; Kohl et al., 2001; Weiler & Black, 2015). The Guiding Model and PIIA, along with use of the associated personally reflective exercises as applied in this case study seem to have done just that, providing interpretation tools that move beyond the information processing type of approach used in guiding to date (Ablett & Dyer, 2009). The guides' self-ratings are thus indicative of critical self-reflection and suggest the capacity and intention to apply what they have learned to their own work as wildlife guides.

One key limitation that must be acknowledged is that the assessment of the guides' capacity to apply knowledge and skills from the training was limited to in-class exercises such as role plays. Follow-up field-based assessment is needed to judge the capacity and commitment of the guides to apply their ecotourism guiding skills and knowledge in their everyday work as swim-with-whale guides.

Ideally, the practical outcomes and effectiveness of this training and interpretive approach need to be assessed *in situ* and comparisons made between trained and untrained guides using methods such as participant observations and tourist responses, however, this is often the most challenging component of this type of research due to logistical and methodological issues (Morgan & Dong, 2008; Weiler & Walker, 2014). More evidence of training uptake and its impacts on tourists and on the sustainability of marine wildlife in Tonga are well beyond the scope of this paper, and we suggest that further research employ mechanisms for evaluating these broader and longer-term training impacts as discussed elsewhere (Kirkpatrick, 1983; Kohl et al., 2001; Weiler & Ham, 2002).

Addressing further research with respect to increased opportunity for more interactive and creative tourism experiences, there is a need to better understand how tourists' expectations of more personal development, enrichment and self-actualisation (Yeoman, 2012) are manifested in wildlife tourism. Curtin (2005, 2009) suggests that wildlife tourists specifically seek more emotionally and spiritually fulfilling outcomes through their interactions and observations of wildlife and immersion in the environment, and makes the distinction that 'experiences are dynamic and emergent; they differ from expectations, and the most memorable and satisfying experiences may be the most unexpected' (2005, p. 1). This implies a more complex analysis of the interaction between the tourist and the guide regarding a mutual determination of the experiential product, outcomes and personal significance, and in so doing involves a situation allied with Binkhorst and Den Dekker's (2009) discussion regarding tourism 'co-creation', where the tourist actively seeks to determine aspects of their own experiences and construct their own personal narratives. Further exploration of the relationships between co-created experiences, memorable outcomes, personal significance and other forms of positive change in the context of guided tours is needed.

Another challenge is to link models, approaches and outcomes with participants' intentional sustainable behaviours beyond the ecotourism experience. Christie and Mason (2003) describe 'transformative tourism' as the 'the practice of organised tourism that leads to a positive change in attitudes and values among those who participate in the tourist experience' (p. 9). In the context of ecotourism, the present study suggests the guide can facilitate the opportunity to see the world differently (Knudson, Cable, & Beck, 1995; Pond, 1993). Skibins, Powell, and Stern (2012) recommend that research address the gaps in our knowledge and provide more detailed examination of how specific guiding and interpretation elements influence both short-term and long-term ecotourism outcomes.

Conclusion and implications

The aims of this paper were to introduce an empirically based training model for guides to respond to the contemporary goals of ecotourism in relation to creating transformative experiential processes, and to examine the outcomes of its application in a training programme. Notwithstanding the limitations of a single case study approach, the findings suggest the Guiding Model and the PIIA, underpinned with appropriate theory and empirical research and methodology, can be effective as training frameworks to help develop critically reflective guides and facilitate positive change in their understanding and knowledge regarding ecotourism and the guide's role in achieving local and global sustainability goals. Hence, this research has implications for the future development and consideration of culturally sensitive and adaptable guide training programmes, their delivery and evaluation, particularly with respect to the rapidly growing attraction and facilitation of marine wildlife ecotourism experiences. There is a need for wider application of these models in other cultural training and guiding contexts, in situations involving both well-developed and developing ecotourism industries.

This study contributes to the tour guiding literature and practice by better understanding the application of numerous psychological and education theories that have been linked to the guide's interpretive role with regard to facilitating effective tourist outcomes, such as identifying and comparing cognitive (knowing or mindful), affective (feeling or emotive) and behavioural (doing) consequences (see Ballantyne, Packer, & Falk, 2011; Ham & Weiler, 2006; Moscardo, 2009). It could be argued that the basis of all these concepts is that for the tourist to act upon new knowledge, feelings, attitudes or perspectives they must be linked to their own significant personal values in order to lead to a sense of responsibility or at least concern, and hence potentially to related subsequent behaviour (Walker & Moscardo, 2014). It is suggested this also applies to the guide with regard to inspiring their sustainable professional conduct, particularly when the ecotourism philosophy is of a Western ideology and possibly not culturally embedded in the guides' personal experience. The principles of the Guiding Model and the PIIA, and their empirical development is that they facilitate the identification and connection of new information and experiences to the individual's personal attitudes, significance and values, with no specific ideological grounds. Hence, the theoretical premise involved in the development and incorporation of these reflective interpretive practices based on the Means-end question approach and cognitive analysis, may contribute to further developing, applying and evaluating the abstract concepts previously discussed. These include seeing Christie and Mason's (2003) transformative tourism notion being actioned, interpreting ecotourism experiences as an opportunity to see the world differently (Knudson et al., 1995) through co-creation opportunities as described by Binkhorst and Den Dekker (2009), and involving the individual's perspective facilitated via the interactive role of the guide and their provocation of such, as long ago proposed by Tilden (1977).

In conclusion, the TWGTP is a government and industry accredited and supported training programme addressing ecotourism principles and empirical research of a contemporary and international standard. It has improved local knowledge, engagement and responsibility regarding the role of the guide and ecotourism from a local to global perspective, and elicited a sense of national pride in leading the way for best practice in whale ecotourism in the South Pacific region. Hence, there are also positive implications of this research and training programme for the sustainability and protection of the endangered South Pacific Humpback whale population, Tonga's Whale Sanctuary, Tonga's major ecotourism industry and the regional communities reliant on its income. As succinctly described by one of the guides, it's …

> Important to do it properly for both the future of the whales as well as for Tonga tourism.

Acknowledgements

We wish to thank the co-trainers John Cvetko and Dr Cara Miller, local translators, tour operators, training participants and all whom helped make this programme a success. The research assistance work of Johanna Schliephack is also gratefully acknowledged.

Disclosure statement

No potential conflict of interest was reported by the authors.

Funding

The Tonga Whale Guide Training Program was funded by the Tonga Business Enterprise Centre who facilitated its delivery in collaboration with Southern Cross University and the University of the South Pacific.

References

Ablett, P. G., & Dyer, P. K. (2009). Heritage and hermeneutics: Towards a broader interpretation of interpretation. *Current Issues in Tourism, 12*(3), 209–233.

Ballantyne, R., & Hughes, K. (2001). Interpretation in ecotourism settings: Investigating tour guides' perceptions of their role, responsibilities and training needs. *Journal of Tourism Studies, 12*(2), 2–9.

Ballantyne, R., & Packer, J. (2011). Using tourism free-choice learning experiences to promote environmentally sustainable behaviour: The role of post-visit 'action' resources'. *Environmental Education Research, 17*(2), 201–215.

Ballantyne, R., & Packer, J. (2013). Ecotourism: Themes and issues. In R. Ballantyne & J. Packer (Eds.), *International handbook on ecotourism* (pp. 1–6). Cheltenham: Edward Elgar.

Ballantyne, R., Packer, J., & Falk, J. (2011). Visitors' learning for environmental sustainability: Testing short- and long-term impacts of wildlife tourism experiences using structural equation modelling. *Tourism Management, 32*, 1243–1252.

Ballantyne, R., Packer, J., & Hughes, K. (2009). Tourists' support for conservation messages and sustainable management practices in wildlife tourism experiences. *Tourism Management, 30*, 658–664.

Ballantyne, R., Packer, J., & Sutherland, L. A. (2011). Visitors' memories of wildlife tourism: Implications for the design of powerful interpretive experiences. *Tourism Management, 32*, 770–779.

Ballantyne, R., & Uzzel, D. (1999). International trends in heritage and environmental interpretation: Future directions for Australian research and practice. *Journal of Interpretation Research, 14*(1), 59–75.

Ballantyne, R., Weiler, B., Crabtree, A., Ham, S. H., & Hughes, K. (2000). *Tour guiding: Developing effective communication and interpretation techniques* [Video and workbook]. Brisbane: Queensland University of Technology.

Binkhorst, E., & Den Dekker, T. (2009). Agenda for co-creation tourism experience research. *Journal of Hospitality Marketing & Management, 18*, 311–327.

Black, R., & King, B. (2002). Human resource development in remote island communities: An evaluation of tour guide training in Vanuatu. *The International Journal of Tourism Research, 4*(2), 103–117.

Black, R., & Weiler, B. (2013). Current themes and issues in ecotour guiding. In R. Ballantyne & J. Packer (Eds.), *International handbook on ecotourism* (pp. 336–350). Cheltenham: Edward Elgar.

Buckley, R. (2013). Defining ecotourism: Consensus on core, disagreement on detail. In R. Ballantyne & J. Packer (Eds.), *International handbook on ecotourism* (pp. 9–14). Cheltenham: Edward Elgar.

Cater, C., & Cater, E. (2007). *Marine ecotourism: Between the devil and the deep blue sea.* Wallingford: CABI.

Ceballos-Lascurin, H. (1996). *Tourism, ecotourism and protected areas.* Gland, Switzerland: IUCN-World Conservation Union.

Christie, M. F., & Mason, P. A. (2003). Transformative tour guiding: Training tour guides to be critically reflective practitioners. *Journal of Ecotourism, 2*(1), 1–16.

Constantine, R., & Bejder, L. (2008). Managing the whale- and dolphin-watching industry: Time for a paradigm shift. In J. Higham & M. Luck (Eds.), *Marine wildlife and tourism management: Insights from the natural and social sciences* (pp. 321–334). Wallingford: CABI.

Cunningham, P. A., Huijbens, E. A., & Wearing, S. L. (2012). From whaling to whale watching: Examining sustainability and cultural rhetoric. *Journal of Sustainable Tourism, 20,* 143–161.

Curtin, S. (2005). Nature, wild animals and tourism: An experiential view. *Journal of Ecotourism, 4*(1), 1–15.

Curtin, S. (2009). Wildlife tourism: The intangible, psychological benefits of human-wildlife encounters. *Current Issues in Tourism, 12*(5–6), 451–474.

Curtin, S. (2010). Managing the wildlife tourism experience: The importance of tour leaders. *International Journal of Tourism Research, 12,* 219–236.

Dobson, J. (2008). Shark! A new frontier in tourist demand for marine wildlife. In J. Higham & M. Luck (Eds.), *Marine wildlife and tourism management: Insights from the natural and social sciences* (pp. 49–65). Wallingford: CABI.

Ham, S. H., & Weiler, B. (2002). Interpretation as the centrepiece of sustainable wildlife tourism. In R. Harris, T. Griffin, & P. Williams (Eds.), *Sustainable tourism: A global perspective* (pp. 35–44). London: Butterworth-Heinemann.

Ham, S. H., & Weiler, B. (2006). *Development of a research-based tool for evaluating interpretation.* Brisbane: Sustainable Tourism Cooperative Centre.

Higginbottom, K. (2004). Wildlife tourism: An introduction. In K. Higginbottom (Ed.), *Wildlife tourism: Impacts, management and planning* (pp. 1–14). Melbourne: Common Ground.

Honey, M. (1999). *Ecotourism and sustainable development: Who owns paradise?* Washington: Island Press.

IFAW. (2009). *Whale watching worldwide: Tourism numbers, expenditures and expanding economic benefits.* Yarmouth: Economists at Large.

Interpretation Australia. (2011). *What is interpretation?* Retrieved October 12, 2011, from http://www.interpretationaustralia.asn.au/about-ia/what-is-interpretation

Jägel, T., Keeling, K., Reppel, A., & Gruber, T. (2012). Individual values and motivational complexities in ethical clothing consumption: A means-end approach. *Journal of Marketing Management, 28*(3–4), 373–396.

Jamal, T., & Camargo, B. A. (2014). Sustainable tourism, justice and an ethic of care: Toward the just destination. *Journal of Sustainable Tourism, 22*(1), 11–30.

Kerstetter, D. L., Jou, J.-S., & Lin, C.-H. (2004). Profiling Taiwanese ecotourists using a behavioural approach. *Tourism Management, 25*(4), 491–498.

Kessler, M., & Harcourt, R. (2010). Aligning tourist, industry and government expectations: A case study from the swim with whales industry in Tonga. *Marine Policy, 34*(6), 1350–1356.

Kim, A. K., Airey, D., & Szivas, E. (2011). The multiple assessment of interpretation effectiveness: Promoting visitors' environmental attitudes and behaviour. *Journal of Travel Research, 50*(3), 321–334.

Kirkpatrick, D. (1983, November). Four steps to measuring training effectiveness. *Personnel Administrator,* pp. 19–25.

Klenosky, D. B., Frauman, E., Norman, W. C., & Gengler, C. E. (1998). Nature-based tourists' use of interpretive services: A means-end investigation. *Journal of Tourism Studies, 9*(2), 26–36.

Knudson, D. M., Cable, T. T., & Beck, L. (1995). *Interpretation of natural and cultural resources.* State College, PA: Venture.

Kohl, J. (2007). Putting the ecotour guide back into context: Using systems thinking to develop quality guides. In R. Black & A. Crabtree (Eds.), *Quality assurance and certification in ecotourism* (pp. 337–363). CABI: Wallingford.

Kohl, J., Brown, C., & Humke, M. (2001). Overcoming hurdles: Teaching guides to interpret biodiversity conservation. *Legacy, 12*(4), 19–28.

Lück, M. (Ed.). (2008). *The encyclopedia of tourism and recreation in marine environments.* Wallingford: CABI.

Mair, J., & Laing, J. H. (2013). Encouraging pro-environmental behaviour: The role of sustainability focused events. *Journal of Sustainable Tourism, 21*(8), 1113–1128.

McArthur, S., & Hall, C. M. (1996). Interpretation: Principles and practice. In C. M. Hall & S. McArthur (Eds.), *Heritage management in Australia and New Zealand: The human dimension* (pp. 88–106). Melbourne: Oxford University Press.

Miller, G., Rathouse, K., Scarles, C., Holmes, K., & Tribe, J. (2010). Public understanding of sustainable tourism. *Annals of Tourism Research, 37*(3), 627–645.

Morgan, M., & Dong, X. D. (2008). Measuring passenger satisfaction of interpretive programming on two Amtrak trains in the Midwest: Testing the expectancy disconfirmation theory. *Journal of Interpretation Research, 13*(2), 43–58.

Moscardo, G. (2009). Understanding tourist experience through mindfulness. In M. Kozak & A. Decrop (Eds.), *Handbook of tourist behaviour: Theory and practice* (pp. 99–115). New York, NY: Routledge.

Moscardo, G. (2013). The role and management of non-captive wildlife in tourism. In R. Ballantyne & J. Packer (Eds.), *International handbook on ecotourism* (pp. 351–364). Cheltenham: Edward Elgar.

Moscardo, G., & Ballantyne, R. (2008). Interpretation and tourist attraction. In A. Fyall, A. Leask, & S. Wanhill (Eds.), *Managing tourist attractions* (2nd ed., pp. 237–252). London: Elsevier.

Moscardo, G., Woods, B., & Saltzer, R. (2004). The role of interpretation in wildlife tourism. In K. Higginbottom (Ed.), *Wildlife tourism: Impacts, management and planning* (pp. 231–252). Melbourne: Common Ground.

Mowforth, M., & Munt, I. (1998). *Tourism and sustainability: New tourism in the third world.* London: Routledge.

Newsome, D., Dowling, R., & Moore, S. (2004). *Wildlife tourism.* Clevedon: Channel View.

Packer, J., & Ballantyne, R. (2013). Encouraging reflective visitor experiences in ecotourism. In R. Ballantyne & J. Packer (Eds.), *International handbook on ecotourism* (pp. 169–177). Cheltenham: Edward Elgar.

Pastorelli, J. (2003). *Enriching the experience – An interpretive approach to tour guiding.* Frenchs Forest: Pearson Education Australia.

Pond, K. (1993). *The professional guide: Dynamics of tour guiding.* New York: VanNostrand Reinhold.

Rodger, K., Moore, S. A., & Newsome, D. (2007). Wildlife tours in Australia: Characteristics, the place of science and sustainable futures. *Journal of Sustainable Tourism, 15*(2), 160–179.

Ross, S., & Wall, G. (2001). Ecotourism: A theoretical framework and an Indonesian application. In S. F. McCool & R. N. Moisey (Eds.), *Tourism, recreation and sustainability: Linking culture and the environment* (pp. 271–288). Oxon: CABI.

Skibins, J. C., Powell, R. B., & Stern, M. J. (2012). Exploring empirical support for interpretation's best practices. *Journal of Interpretation Research, 17*(1), 25–44.

Smith, V. L. (2001). Sustainability. In V. L. Smith & M. Brent (Eds.), *Hosts and guests revisited* (pp. 187–200). New York, NY: Cognizant Communication.

TIES. (2015). *What is ecotourism?* Retrieved May 20, 2015, from https://www.ecotourism.org/what-is-ecotourism

Tilden, F. (1977). *Interpreting our heritage.* Chapel Hill: University of North Carolina Press.

Tsang, N. K., Yeung, S., & Cheung, C. (2011). A critical investigation of the use and effectiveness of interpretive services. *Asia Pacific Journal of Tourism Research, 16*(2), 123–137.

Walker, K. (2007). *The role of interpretation in sustainable tourism: A qualitative approach to understanding passenger experiences on Expedition Cruises* (PhD thesis). James Cook University, Townsville Qld.

Walker, K., & Hawkins, E. (2013). Watching and swimming with marine mammals: International scope, management and best practice in cetacean ecotourism. In R. Ballantyne & J. Packer (Eds.), *International handbook on ecotourism* (pp. 365–381). Cheltenham: Edward Elgar.

Walker, K., & Moscardo, G. (2011). Controversial ecotourism and stakeholder roles in governance: 'Swim with Humpback whales' in Vava'u. In E. Laws, H. Richins, J. Agrusa, & N. Scott (Eds.), *Tourism destination governance: Practice, theory and issues* (pp. 103–116). Wallingford: CABI.

Walker, K., & Moscardo, G. (2014). Encouraging sustainability beyond the tourist experience: Ecotourism, interpretation and values. *Journal of Sustainable Tourism, 22*(8), 1175–1196.

Walker, K., Weiler, B., & Cvetko, J. (2012). *The Tonga whale guide training program evaluation report*. Lismore, NSW: Southern Cross University.

Wearing, S., & Neil, J. (1999). *Ecotourism: Impacts, potentials and possibilities*. Oxford: Butterworth-Heinemann.

Weaver, D. B. (2001). Introduction to ecotourism. In D. B. Weaver (Ed.), *The encyclopedia of ecotourism* (pp. 1–3). Wallingford: CABI.

Weaver, D. B., & Lawton, L. J. (2007). Twenty years on: The state of contemporary ecotourism research. *Tourism Management, 28*(5), 1168–1179.

Weiler, B., & Black, R. (2015). *Tour guiding research: Insights, issues and implications*. Bristol: Channel View.

Weiler, B., & Ham, S. (2002). Tour guide training: A model for sustainable capacity building in developing countries. *Journal of Sustainable Tourism, 10*(1), 52–69.

Weiler, B., & Ham, S. H. (2001). Tour guides and interpretation. In D. B. Weaver (Ed.), *The encyclopedia of ecotourism* (pp. 549–563). Wallingford: CABI.

Weiler, B., & Walker, K. (2014). Enhancing the visitor experience: Reconceptualising the tour guide's communicative role. *Journal of Hospitality & Tourism Management, 21*, 90–99.

Yeoman, I. (2012). *2050 – tomorrow's tourism*. Bristol: Channel View.

Watching wildlife in Cabo Polonio, Uruguay: tourist control or auto-control?

Carme Tuneu Corral, Diana Szteren and Marcelo H. Cassini

ABSTRACT

Cabo Polonio (Uruguay) is a popular but atypical centre for beach vacations, because tourists spend days without electricity, running water and vehicle. There is a continental pinniped colony that acts as secondary attraction, but there is not direct control over tourist visits to the rookery. Our objective was to evaluate the experience of visitors to this pinniped colony. We used questionnaires to determine the information used by tourists and to analyse their attitudes towards the colony conservation. To validate questionnaires, we also conducted direct observations of the tourist-pinniped interactions. Less than 15% of tourists received information, which was provided by local people. Most tourists saw the rookery as an important touristic attraction. There was total consensus about the requirement for wildlife information. Despite the lack of active supervision, most people behaved properly and complied with conservation measures: the probability that a tourist crossed the fence during a visit was only 0.002 (17 crosses in 902 hours). This positive attitude is possible related to the fact that tourists in Cabo Polonio, accept the discomfort of living without social commodities and welcome the closeness with nature. It is expected that most people will have a spontaneous predisposition to take care of nature.

Introduction

Tourism is one of the world's largest industries and has seen an average annual increase of 6.6% since the 1960s (Yeoman, Munro, & McMahon-Beattie, 2006). Nature-based tourism is no exception. It has been defined as tourism focused principally on natural resources such as relatively undisturbed parks and natural areas, wetlands, wildlife reserves and other areas of protected flora, fauna and habitats (Laarman & Durst, 1993; Weaver, 2006). Wildlife-watching tourism is a type of ecotourism that should be distinguished from other forms of wildlife tourism, such as captive-wildlife, hunting and fishing tourism (Higginbottom, 2004; Newsome, Dowling, & Moore, 2004). In a recent study using viability population analysis, Buckley, Morrison, and Castley (2016) showed that wildlife tourism can extend expected survival time for some species; however, it does not currently overcome other major conservation threats associated with natural resource extractive industries. The increase in this type of tourism demands ecological research on its potential negative effects on wildlife and socio-psychological research on its potential positive effects in relation to other anthropogenic threats such as poaching, primary industries and habitat loss (Fennell, 2015; Steven & Castley, 2013).

Marine mammals are charismatic animals that are frequently found around accessible coastal areas of the world (Jefferson, Leatherwood, & Webber, 1993). This has resulted in financially viable businesses based on taking tourists to see them and led to a rapid growth in marine mammal-based tourism (Constantine, 1999). There are concerns over the impacts of this growing industry on the conservation of species, and therefore research has been conducted to evaluate the effect of tourism on the behaviour, demography and ecology of marine mammals (Barton, Booth, Ward, Simmons, & Fairweather, 1998; Curtin, Richards, & Westcott, 2009; Orsini, Shaughnessy, & Newsome, 2006).

More than 20 years ago, we initiated a study on the impact of tourists on a colony of the South American fur seal *Arctocephalus australis* and the sea lion *Otaria flavescens* in Cabo Polonio National Park, Uruguay (Cassini, 2001; Cassini, Szteren, & Fernández-Juricic, 2004). The main goal of our research was to establish the impact of tourist approaches on the behaviour and distribution of the animals of this colony. We found that the most disturbing effects were produced by large groups, approaches closer than 10 meters, and intrusive tourist behaviour. In other words, in previous studies, we analysed the interaction tourists-pinnipeds from the point of view of the animals. In this paper, we analysed this interaction from the point of view of the tourists.

Uruguay is a very interesting case study for tourism (Brida, Scuderi, & Seijas, 2014). The tourism industry has become a key sector of the Uruguayan economy, both for its importance in generating value-added and job creation and as a generator of foreign exchange (Brida et al., 2014). Over the past decade, the tourism sector generated revenue of currency similar to that generated by traditional exports, reaching between 20% and 30% of foreign exchange generated by total exports and equivalent to 3% of gross domestic product (Brida et al., 2014).

Cabo Polonio is an atypical National Park in several ways. It is the first National Park of Uruguay despite being created as recently as 2009. At present, the village is a beach touristic centre, but its origin is very different. It was created around the exploitation and killing of sea lions organized by a government institution called 'Industrias Loberas y Pesqueras del Estado' (State Industries for fish and Sea Lion Exploitation). Cabo Polonio was the last place to practice legal and systematic killing of marine mammals in South America.

The village is small, with around 200 'ranchos', small and simple houses used by tourists as temporary residences. However, in summer, the influx of people is enormous, with more than 30,000 tourists entering Cabo Polonio in January alone (Cabo Polonio National Park records, personal communication), in search of its wonderful beaches.

The most important characteristic of the village is its lack of electricity, running water and roads in or leading to it. Currently, solar energy devices are being set up in some ranchos but for decades tourists have depended on candles for nocturnal illumination and water was obtained by collecting rain or from 'cachimbas', simple holes in the sand that access fresh ground water. The village is reached by walking or in four-wheeled trucks some of them recycled from the Second World War.

At the tip of the Cape there is a lighthouse. A colony of pinnipeds is established in the rookery below it. This colony consists of males unable to obtain breeding sites on three islands located in front of Cabo Polonio' (Vaz Ferreira & Ponce de León, 1984). The peak in tourist numbers coincides with the breeding season, when pinnipeds congregate on the islands, and is consequently when the highest number of animals is found at the continental colony. The rooky continental haul out is freely visited by tourists. There is no oversight of this activity, so people can observe the animals whenever and for as long as they desire. In 1997, a wire fence was installed and remains the only management strategy designed to limit human access to the colony (Cassini et al., 2004). Despite some boards with a 'no trespassing' warning are attached, the fence is easily scaled, so it serves mainly as a symbolic limit rather than an actual restriction.

Cabo Polonio should be considered a typical 3S (sun, sea, sand) touristic site, with people emphasis on hedonism and massive search for its sea, sand and sun during the summer. There are no guided tours to visit the pinniped colonies or any other wildlife-watching service. There are no scientific outreach channels towards the tourism structure. The only exception is a small information centre with almost no information about the pinnipeds biology, which is located outside the Cabo, where people take the transport for entering the Park. Stable population is less than one hundred people. During the summer, they are mainly occupied in providing services to the thousands of tourists that arrive, preparing food, serving in the few general stores available in the town, cleaning houses or selling handicrafts. Even with all these enormous limitations that appear to prevent a truly ecotouristic approach, Cabo Polonio is a unique place because of the decision of the community (locals and tourists) of living without modern comfort, regardless of cars, electricity or running water.

Our objective was to evaluate the experience of visitors to the pinniped continental colony in Cabo Polonio National Park. We used questionnaires to determine the information used by tourists and their attitudes towards the conservation of the colony, including their experience of approaching the animals. We tested two contrasting hypotheses: (1) lack of guards providing information and controlling tourist behaviour, produces an inadequate response of most tourists that threatens the sustainability of wildlife-watching tourism in Cabo Polonio and (2) tourist auto-control is a widespread phenomenon in Cabo Polonio, due to the exceptional characteristics of this touristic site that predispose visitors to take care of nature and wildlife. In the latter case, sustainability can be still threatened because, even when most tourists might behave properly, the impact of inadequate behaviour of a few can be enormous.

Materials and methods

Cabo Polonio National Park (34°24′S, 53°46′W) is located in north-east Uruguay. In the last few years, it has been one of the most visited beach tourist centres of the country with a total of 81,205 visitors in 2015 (unpublished data of the National Park Administration). The park consists of a portion of coast, an oceanic sector and islands within the latter, totalling 25,820 hectares. The town of Cabo Polonio is located inside the park. The climate of the region is humid subtropical with maritime features, presenting well-marked seasonal variations in temperature as well as a risk of prolonged drought. Between July and August, temperatures are at their lowest and maximum temperatures are recorded in January (Chouhy, 2013; Panario & Gutiérrez, 2005). Rainfall is more abundant during winter, with an annual average of 1277 mm; the average annual temperature is 16.4°C.

Convenience sampling method was used to collect data for this study. We conducted an on-site survey among visitors to Cabo Polonio from November 2014 to February 2015. The only way to leave Cabo Polonio (apart from walking) is in 4×4 trucks that depart every half-hour from a point in the centre of the village. In the evening, large groups of tourists wait there for a truck in which to leave the National Park. A semi-structured questionnaire was administered to a random sample of visitors waiting for the arrival of the trucks during November and December 2014, and another semi-structured questionnaire was administered during January and February 2015 (Appendix). Data were collected using a survey questionnaire written in Spanish. Once selected and approached, an individual was invited to respond orally to the questionnaire. Nobody rejected to participate in the interview. All interviews were conducted by the same interviewer: C.T.C. The questionnaire had a simple design. Finally, a total of 25 questions from the two questionnaires were analysed, and 84% had a yes/no type of answer.

This interview was designed to assess the degree of information they had about pinniped biology, the type of information that should be provided in the future, their reasons for visiting this pinniped continental colony and possible ways of improving it. Due to the descriptive nature of the study and the simplicity of the questionnaire, there were no statistical analyses applied to data, and results are presented as percentage of total responses.

From 20 November 2014 to 5 February 2015 and from 08:00 to 19:00, we also conducted direct observations of the behaviour of tourists and sea lions during the visits. Most of the results of this study will be part of another manuscript and published elsewhere, however here we report results on frequency of visits and number of times that tourists crossed the fence. These data provide with a validation of the information provided by tourists during interviews.

Results

From November to December, 60 interviews were conducted, and 47 more were conducted during January and February. The results of these interviews are shown in Table 1. The majority of tourists were visiting Cabo Polonio for the first time (57.4%), but a large number was already familiar with the area. Almost all tourists (95.0%) visited the colony. The average length of the visit was 45 min and the average group size was 2.2 people. The great majority were seeing a pinniped colony for the first time (92.2%). The vast majority declared they had not jumped the fence (96.7%). These results enable characterization of the visits and visitor profiles.

Information available for tourists was poor. Not one of the tourists had received expert information, that is, they did not interact with park guards or guides, received no brochures or other sources of supervised material. Less than 15% of tourists received information from local people, mainly hostel owners or the lighthouse keepers, who are Uruguayan soldiers. More than half of the tourists did not know that Cabo Polonio was

Table 1. Questionnaire results.

Responses	Mean
Data on the visit	
Days in Cabo Polonio (SD)	7.8 (17.7)
First time in Cabo Polonio	57.4%
The interviewee visited the continental rookery	92.2%; 97.9%[a]
Minutes of the visit (SD)	45.8 (30.2); 43.3 (26.4)[a]
Group size (SD)	2.2 (1.2)
The colony was the preferred attraction (vs. lighthouse, village, beaches)	23.4%
The interviewee crossed the fence	3.3%
The interviewee had visited other pinniped colonies	19.1%
Opinion	
The presence of people disturbs the animals	29.8%
Pinnipeds can cause damage to local people (e.g. artisanal fishery)	8.5%
The colony is an important touristic attraction of Cabo Polonio	97.9%
There is a risk in getting too close to the animals	27.7%
The level of protection (i.e. the fence) is excessive	4.3%
Handling information	
The interviewee did not know about the colony before arrival	40.4%
The interviewee received information from local people	13.3%; 14.9%
The interviewee received information (from guards or brochures, etc.)	0%; 0%
The interviewee knew that Cabo Polonio is a National Park	42.6%
The interviewee knew that there are thousands of pinnipeds in the islands	33.3%
The interviewee knew how many species of pinnipeds are in Cabo Polonio	13.3%
The interviewee knew what the animals do during the summer	3.3%
Tourist suggestions	
The interviewee would like to approach the animals more	11.7%
The interviewee would like to receive more information on local wildlife	100%
Tourists should be aware of the risk of approaching too closely to pinnipeds	100%
The interviewee would like to receive information in brochures or posters	100%
The interviewee would like an information centre close to the colony	100%

[a]The question was included in the questionnaires of November/December 2014 and January/March 2015.

a National Park, assuming that it was a village associated with beach enjoyment like others on the Uruguayan coast. The majority did not know how many species of pinnipeds live in the area (86.7%), nor that the islands contain large colonies (57.4%), and only 3.3% knew that these colonies serve for species reproduction.

In relation to tourist opinions, experience and expectations, most people saw the rookery as an important touristic attraction of Cabo Polonio (97.9%), while it was the most preferred one for 23.4%. The ranking of preference was: south beach, lighthouse, rookery, north beach and village, suggesting that the observation of pinnipeds was preferred over the use of one of the two sandy beaches available in Cabo Polonio.

There was total consensus (100%) about the requirement for information on wildlife, natural ecosystems and the cultural traditions of the region, and more specifically on pinniped biology. Furthermore, responses to the possibility of building an interpretation centre inside the cape, so tourists could receive information *in situ*, were 100% positive.

Another conclusive result provided by interviews was the tourists' opinion in relation to the level of protection of the continental rookery. Almost all of them (95.7%) considered that there was an adequate level of protection, that is, they accepted the existence of a fence that kept the animals at a distance. This point of view was maintained even though most of them believed that human presence did not disturb the animals (29.8%) and that pinnipeds were not dangerous when approached at close quarters (27.7%).

A total of 902 hours of observations of tourists and sea lions at the colony were conducted. During November and December 2014, a total of 1059 visits to the colony were recorded. During the January and February, the presence of tourist in the colony was almost constant, so it was impossible to count separated visits. During the total study period, only 17 times, tourists crossed the fence (there were another 77 instances of tourists approaching sea lions and less than 10 meters in sector that did not have the fence, so it is not relevant to the purpose of validation of interviews).

Discussion

A large number of wildlife populations suitable for tourist visitors are located in low- and medium-income countries. Economic and political difficulties often limit the possibilities of developing strategies for sustainable management of nature-based tourism in these countries. Research on the expectations, attitudes, knowledge and behaviour of tourists is relatively cheap and affordable even with low financial resources and may provide information that facilitates the definition of priorities and action plans in these countries.

This study is the first attempt at analysing the human dimension of the activity of wildlife viewing tourism in Uruguay. Cabo Polonio is, at the same time, one of the most famous and popular resorts, the first National Park, and one of the most biodiverse spots in the country.

Cabo Polonio has an efficient entrance system, and by park guards are usually oriented to this control. Other functions of the administration are related to camping control and other policing functions. In contrast, educational and recreational functions are almost absent. Our results showed clearly the lack of information available for the people that visit Cabo Polonio. They arrived at the rookery without knowing how to behave and about the risks to the animals or themselves if they scaled the fence that surrounds the colony. Most of them were ignorant of basic information on the animals they were observing, including the number of species. Many tourists spent several days in the area without even knowing that it was a National Park. Level of specialization has been used as a core dimension for categorizing and describing different visitors in wildlife situations (Moscardo & Saltzer, 2004). Based on the results of this study, visits to the continental rookery of Cabo Polonio can be considered an extreme case of novices/generalists form of wildlife-watching tourism (Duffus & Dearden, 1990).

Some visitors were aware of the situation and demanded more information; they agreed with the idea of creating an information centre in the village close to the colony. One type of management response on the tourist pressure increase, related on the natural environment, lies in educating tourist (Orams, 1996). Several publications include planning frameworks for interpretation (e.g. Ham, 1992; Knudson, Cable, & Beck, 1995; Sharpe, 1982). A number of these approaches could be utilized in developing an interpretative programme in Cabo Polonio.

Ecotourism involves multiple initiatives with a wide range of characteristics which were clearly described by Weaver (2005) who classified them into hard and soft types. In addition, the economic benefit for local community is also one of the key factors which define any ecotourism proposal. Therefore, considering the social characteristics of this wildlife spot, the communitybased tourism approach could be another notion to explore. All of these notions could reinforce the strategy of the truly sustainable tourism initiative into a protected area like Cabo Polonio.

In relation to tourist attitudes, even when people travelled to Cabo Polonio mainly to make use of its exceptional beaches, almost all of them visited the pinniped colony and found it to be an important touristic attraction. A relatively large proportion of people found the rookery even more enjoyable than the beaches. They spent a relatively long time observing the animals, even when they did not receive any information on how to make the most of their visit. For a large proportion of tourists, it was their first experience of close interaction with marine mammals. Therefore, we may conclude that Cabo Polonio offers a unique opportunity for improving knowledge of and sensitivity towards marine mammal conservation issues.

Despite the lack of available information and authority presence, most visitors respected the animals and were also supportive of protective measures. Only a very small proportion of people scaled the fence; the majority did not approach it and preferred to observe the animals from a distance. Almost everybody agreed with the presence of the fence and preferred not to approach the animals any closer. Data on direct observation of tourist behaviour validated these results of the interviews: only a few visitors cross the fence, with a total of 0.002 crosses per hour of observation. However, it is worth taking into account that approaches to the animals in areas without fence occurred and can have significant negative consequences to the colony.

In summary, visitors were supportive of protective measures and behaved accordingly. There are at least two possible explanations of this positive attitude. The first one is that the fence acts as an effective deterrent of irresponsible behaviour. The second and the more probable is related to the atypical socio-cultural nature of Cabo Polonio. People who spend their holidays there accept the discomfort and welcome the communal experience of closeness with nature. It is not something undertaken by only a few very experienced travellers that reach remote places of the world, but attracts massive numbers of tourists searching for a summer holiday on the beach. In this sense, Cabo Polonio is a unique place that deserves to be investigated as a phenomenon of truly sustainable tourism. In this socio-cultural context, it is expected that most people will have a spontaneous predisposition to take care of nature, including colonies of pinnipeds.

Unfortunately, this positive attitude of the majority does not prevent some visitors climbing over the fence and upsetting the animals, with negative consequences for the colony. In a study conducted the year after the erection of the fence, Cassini et al. (2004) showed that the most stressful pinniped behavioural responses had been reduced, but tourists still approached the animals, affecting the behaviour and distribution of the animals.

In summary, this study showed clear trends in the human dimension of tourist-pinniped interactions in Cabo Polonio: there is no control over the interactions, tourists receive little information to guide their visit, and most people behave properly and respect conservation measures. It is recommended that the National Park administration develops an interpretation programme and provides staff *in situ* to prevent approaches to the animals by tourists, informing people about the species and the park, and stimulating positive attitudes towards marine mammal conservation issues.

Geolocation information

Cabo Polonio National Park, Uruguay (34°24′S, 53°46′W).

Disclosure statement

No potential conflict of interest was reported by the authors.

References

Barton, K., Booth, K. L., Ward, J. C., Simmons, D. G., & Fairweather, J. R. (1998). *Visitor and New Zealand fur seal interactions along the Kaikoura coast.* (Tourism Research and Education Centre, Report No. 9). Canterbury: Lincoln University.
Brida, J. G., Scuderi, R., & Seijas, M. N. (2014). Segmenting cruise passengers visiting Uruguay: A factor–cluster analysis. *International Journal of Tourism Research, 16*, 209–222.
Buckley, R. C., Morrison, C., & Castley, J. G. (2016). Net effects of ecotourism on threatened species survival. *PLoS ONE, 11*(2), e0147988. doi:10.1371/journal.pone.0147988
Cassini, M. H. (2001). Behavioural responses of South American fur seals to approach by tourists – A brief report. *Applied Animal Behaviour Science, 71*, 341–346.
Cassini, M., Szteren, D., & Fernández-Juricic, E. (2004). Fence effects on the behavioural responses of South American fur seals to tourist approaches. *Journal of Ethology, 22*, 127–133.
Chouhy, M. (2013). Cabo Polonio, área protegida: conservacionismo en diálogo con cosmovisiones salvajes. *Anuario de Antropología Social y Cultural en Uruguay, 11*, 87–102.
Constantine, R. (1999). *Effects of tourism on marine mammals in New Zealand.* Science for Conservation 106. Wellington: Department of Conservation.
Curtin, S. C., Richards, S., & Westcott, S. M. (2009). Tourism and grey seals in south Devon: Management strategies, voluntary controls and tourists' perceptions of disturbance. *Current Issues in Tourism, 12*(1), 59–81.
Duffus, D. A., & Dearden, P. (1990). Non-consumptive wildlife-oriented recreation: A conceptual framework. *Biological Conservation, 53*, 213–231.
Fennell, D. A. (2015). *Ecotourism* (4th ed.). London: Routledge.
Ham, S. H. (1992). *Environmental interpretation: A practical guide for people with big ideas and small budgets.* Golden, CO: North American Press.
Higginbottom, K. (2004). Wildlife tourism: An introduction. In K. Higginbottom (Ed.), *Wildlife tourism: Impacts, management and planning* (pp. 1–14). Gold Coast: Common Ground Publishing, CRC for Sustainable Tourism.
Jefferson, T. A., Leatherwood, S., & Webber, M. A. (1993). *Marine mammals of the world – FAO species identification guide.* Rome: Food and Agriculture Organization of the United Nations.
Knudson, D. M., Cable, T. T., & Beck, L. (1995). *Interpretation of cultural and natural resources.* State College, PA: Venture Publishing.
Laarman, J. G., & Durst, P. B. (1993). Nature tourism as a tool for economic development and conservation of natural resources. In J. Nenon, & P. B. Durst (Eds.), *Nature tourism in Asia: Opportunities and constraints for conservation and economic development* (pp. 1–19). Washington, DC: US Forest Service.
Moscardo, G., & Saltzer, R. (2004). Understanding wildlife tourism markets. In K. Higginbottom (Ed.), *Wildlife tourism: Impacts, management and planning* (pp. 167–186). Altona: Common Ground Publishing Pty Ltd and Cooperative Research Centre for Sustainable Tourism.
Newsome, D., Dowling, R., & Moore, S. (2004). *Wildlife tourism.* Cleveland: Channel View Publications.
Orams, M. B. (1996). Using interpretation to manage nature-based tourism. *Journal of Sustainable Tourism, 4*, 81–94.
Orsini, J. P., Shaughnessy, P. D., & Newsome, D. (2006). Impacts of human visitors on Australian sea lions (*Neophoca cinerea*) at Carnac Island, Western Australia: Implications for Tourism Management. *Tourism in Marine Environments, 3*, 101–115.
Panario, D., & Gutiérrez, O. (2005). La vegetación en la evolución de playas arenosas. *El caso de la costa uruguaya. Ecosistemas, 14*, 150–161.
Sharpe, G. W. (1982). *Interpreting the environment.* New York, NY: John Wiley & Sons Inc.

Steven, R., & Castley, J. G. (2013). Tourism as a threat to critically endangered and endangered birds: Global patterns and trends in conservation hotspots. *Biodiversity and Conservation, 22*, 1063–1082.

Vaz Ferreira, R., & Ponce de León, A. (1984). Estudios sobre *Arctocephalus australis* (Zimmermann, 1783), lobo de dos pelos Sudamericano. *Universidad de la República, Uruguay, 1*, 1–18.

Weaver, D. B. (2005). Comprehensive and minimalist dimensions of ecotourism. *Annals of Tourism Research, 32*(2), 439–455.

Weaver, D. B. (2006). *Sustainable tourism: Theory and practice.* Oxford: Butterworth-Heinemann.

Yeoman, I., Munro, C., & McMahon-Beattie, U. (2006). Tomorrow's: World, consumer and tourist. *Journal of Vacation Marketing, 12*, 174–190.

Appendix: Questionnaire, original in Spanish

I. Questionnaire of November/December 2014

a. Did you visit the sea lion colony? If you didn't visit it, ¿it was because you were not interested, because you didn't have time or because you didn't know about it?

b. If you visited it, ¿How much time did you remain there (min.)? How was the size of your group (number of persons)?

c. Did you cross the fence, did you approach the boundary of the fence, or did you see the animals from the rocks (behind the fence)?

d. Did you see animals outside of the protected area? How many?

e. During your stay here, did you receive any type of information about the fur seal colony? Who provided you this information? Could you tell me some of it?

f. Do you know what is in the islands in front of the Cape?

g. Do you know how many species of fur seals live in Cabo Polonio?

h. Do you know what are sea lions doing in the rockery and in the islands in front of the Cape during the summer?

i. Would you like to get closer to the animals or, in the other hand, do you think that we would have to give them more protection with a fence which could not be crossed?

j. Would you like that more information about fauna and flora from Cabo Polonio was available?

k. Do you think that is necessary to alert tourists about the risks of approaching sea lions, both for the tourists and animals?

II. Questionnaire of January/February 2015

a. How much time have you spent in Cabo Polonio (days)?

b. Is the first time that you visit Cabo Polonio?

c. Which places have you visited? (South beach, North beach, lighthouse, colony, village)

d. Which places you like more?

e. How did you know about the existence of the sea lion colony? (Once here, before arriving here)

f. Have you received any information about sea lions? Who gave you it?

g. Have you visited other sea lion colonies in Uruguay or in other countries?

h. How long have you been watching sea lions (min.)?

i. Do you think that the human presence disturb sea lions?

j. Do you think that sea lions can damage a local activity (e.g. local fishery)?

k. Do you think that the colony is an important tourist attraction of Cabo Polonio?

l. Do you think that there is any risk in getting too close of the animals?

m. Do you think that protection level is sufficient, insufficient or excessive?

n. Would you like receiving more information about sea lions in brochures or posters?

o. Do you know that Cabo Polonio is a Natural Park?

p. Would you like to have an interpretation centre in Cabo Polonio with information about its nature and culture?

Index

Note: Page numbers in *italics* refer to figures
Page numbers in **bold** refer to tables

African Safari Lodge Foundation (ASLF) 52
African Wildlife Foundation (AWF) 35
Agrawal, A. 49
agriculture, transformation of 37–9, **38**
agritourism, benefits of 5
agroecology 4–5
agroecotourism 1; benefits 5; community
   capitals framework (CCF) 7–18; community
   development through 3–18; Cuban 7;
   defined 5; on farm 17–18; impacts 15–18; as
   niche market 18; post revolution Cuban
   agriculture 6–7
Armstrong, R. 50
Ashley, C. 50, 62

Bebbington, A. 27
Best, Mechelle 3
Binkhorst, E. 84, 86
biodiversity conservation 49
Black, R. 70, 73, 74
Botswana Tourism Organization (BTO) 34
Bramwell, B. 24
Bregendahl, C. 27
Bricker, Kelly S. 1
Buckley, R. C. 91–2
Budowski, G. 25
buffer zones 34, 35
built capital 15, *26*; before/after ecotourism
   adoption **33**; overview of **8, 27**; visual aide
   of *11*
business-community partnerships 51–2, 58

Cabo Polonio (Uruguay): behaviour of tourists
   and sea lions during visits 94–6; positive
   attitudes towards marine mammal
   conservation issues 97; watching wildlife in
   91–7
capital: assets 25; categories of **8**, 25, 26, *26*, **27**;
   defined 8; *see also specific entries*
Carter, E. 25

cash economy, through ecotourism 36–7, 40
Cassini, Marcelo H. 91
Castley, J. G. 91–2
Castro, Raul 7, 18
Cavaliere, C. 18
Ceballos-Lascuráin, H. 48
Children in the Wilderness 61
Chobe Enclave Conservation Trust (CECT):
   authority 37; development of 35; in
   ecotourism project 25, 29–30; formation of 34
Chobe Wildlife Trust 32
Christ, C. 40
Christie, M. F. 73–4, 85, 86
co-creation tourism 84, 86
commoditisation, of culture 37
community capitals framework (CCF) 1;
   agroecotourism and 7–18; changes, after
   ecotourism 32–5, **33**; community assets
   within **8**; and community needs 28;
   development 8; ecotourism and 25–8;
   implementation 4; outcomes *26*; stock and
   flow impact 25, 27–8; visual aide and
   explanation 10, *11*; *see also* capital
community development, through
   agroecotourism, in Cuba 3–18
community empowerment, measuring 27
community needs, changes in: agriculture
   transformation 37–9; cash flow prevalence
   36–7; CCF and 28
community resources, types of *11*
Conservation International (CI) 52
controlled hunting areas (CHAs) 29, 34
Corral, Carme Tuneu 91
crop production 30, **38**
Cuba, agroecotourism in 3–18
cultural capital 12, 15, *26*; before/after
   ecotourism adoption **33**; overview of **8, 27**;
   visual aide of *11*
cumulative causation, theory of 8
Curtin, S. 84

De Witt, L. 49
Den Dekker, T. 84, 86
Denzin, N. 31
Department of Wildlife and National Parks
   (DWNP) 32, 34
Duffy, Lauren N. 3

ecoorganic tourism 5
ecotourism 1–2; and biodiversity 40; cash flow
   prevalence 36–7; changes in community
   capitals after 32–5, **33**; changes in community
   needs 36–9; Chobe Enclave Conservation
   Trust (CECT, study area) 25, 29–30;
   community capitals framework (CCF) 25–8;
   data collection and analysis 30–2; defined 48,
   72; development 23; experiences 76;
   household income from 57, **57**; income
   generation 35, 50, 92; influencing on
   community needs and functions of PAs
   22–42; interpretation as element in 72; key
   principles 49; methods and findings 29–39;
   role in local socio-economic development
   49–50; stakeholders 50–2, **51**; sustainability
   goals 72–3; system thinking approach in
   23–5; training approach for guides 69–86;
   transformation of agriculture 37–9;
   wildlife-based 32–4, 69–70; *see also* guides;
   private sector ecotourism; wildlife-watching
   tourism
Emery, M. F. 8
employment opportunities, and capacity
   building: through skills training and
   development 55–7
Epler Wood International 52

farm tourism 5
Fennell, D. 48
Fey, S. 27
financial capital 14–15, 17, *26*; before/
   after ecotourism adoption **33**; from
   ecotourism 36–7; overview of **8, 27**;
   visual aide of *11*
Flora, C. 8, 25–7
food shortages 6
fur seals (*Arctocephalus australis*) 92

gender equality 14
Goodwin, H. 61, 63
Grand Circle Foundation 61
gross domestic product 7, 92
guides: development of Guiding Model 74–6,
   75; ecotourism training 73–4; important
   training outcomes 79–83, **81–2**; pre- and
   post-training survey 79, *80*; responses to
   questions 79, *80*; role/responsibility, in
   sustainable wildlife tourism 72–3, 79, *80*, **81**;
   Tonga Whale Guide Training Program
   (TWGTP) 71, 76–8, 86; training approach
   for 69–86

Guiding Model 74–6, *75*
Gutierrez-Montes, I. 8

Hall, D. 41
Hierarchical Value Map (HVM) 74
household income, from ecotourism 57, **57**
human capital 12–13, 16, *26*; before/after
   ecotourism adoption **33**; overview of **8, 27**;
   visual aide of *11*
human–wildlife conflicts 32, 34, 38–9
hunting tourism 29, 34

indirect employment 56
Industrias Loberas y Pesqueras del Estado
   (State Industries for fish and Sea Lion
   Exploitation) 92
infrastructural developments, in remote areas
   59
Integrated Rural Development and Nature
   Conservation (IRDNC) 52
International Union for Conservation of
   Nature 71
interpretation, defined 72

job opportunities, in remote areas 55
joint ventures (JVs), creation of 58
Jones, S. 27

Kalahari Conservation Society (KCS) 32
Kerstetter, Deborah L. 1
King, B. 70
Kline, Carol 3

Land Use and Management Plan, for buffer
   zones 35
Lane, B. 24
Laverack, G. 27
leakages, from tourism 49–50, *50*
lease fee payments 58, **60**
Lenao, M. 24
Lincoln, Y. 31
local linkages/value chains development 59

marine mammal-based tourism 92
Mason, P. A. 73–4, 85, 86
McKinnon, Hunt 3
means-end question approach 76
modern housing, transition to 36
Morrison, C. 91–2
Moscardo, G. 72
Myrdal, G. 8

Namibian Association of CBNRM
   Organisations (NACSO) 52
National Park of Uruguay *see* Cabo Polonio
   (Uruguay)
natural capital 11–12, 16, *26*, 32; before/after
   ecotourism adoption **33**; overview of **8, 27**;
   visual aide of *11*

nature-based tourism 22, 48, 91
Nyaupane, Gyan P. 22

organipónicos 4, 6; and community,
    investigation 9–11
organisational changes 28

Personal Insight Interpretive Approach (PIIA)
    70, 75
philanthropic donations 59–60, 62
photographic tourism 29, 34
physical capital see built capital
political capital 13–14, 17, 26; before/after
    ecotourism adoption 33; overview of 8, 27;
    visual aide of 11
post revolution Cuban agriculture 6–7
poverty reduction, and local socio-economic
    development 49
Powell, R. B. 85
private sector ecotourism: employment
    opportunities and capacity building 55–7;
    infrastructure development 59; joint
    ventures (JVs) 58; leakages from 49–50, 50;
    lease fees, payment of 58, 60; local linkages/
    value chains development 59; in local
    socio-economic development, southern
    Africa 47–64; NGO's role in developments
    52; philanthropy/donations 59–60, 62;
    stakeholders engaging in 50–2, 51;
    Wilderness Safaris (WS) company 52–3
protected areas (PAs): acceptance of tourism
    industry 24; challenge for 40–1; linkage
    through tourism development 22–3;
    sustainability of 40
public–private partnerships 48

Redford, K. 49
revenue generation, in ecotourism 35, 50, 92
Roberts, L. 41
Roe, E. 50
rural community development 50, 63

Saayman, M. 49
Saggers, S. 27
Salafsky, N. 25
Sandbrook, C. G. 49
Save the Rhino Trust (SRT) 52
sea lions (Otaria flavescens) 92
Serageldin, I. 27
Sharpley, R. 24
Skibins, J. C. 85
skills training, and development: employment
    opportunities through 55–7
Snyman, S. 47, 55
social capital 13, 17, 26, 32, 39; before/after
    ecotourism adoption 33; overview of 8, 27;
    visual aide of 11
socio-economic impact, on local communities
    see private sector ecotourism

South Africa: private sector ecotourism in
    47–64
'Special Period in a Time of Peace', in Cuba 6
Spenceley, A. 50, 61, 63
'spiralling-up', idea of 8, 16
stakeholders, participation in ecotourism 50–2,
    51
State Industries for fish and Sea Lion
    Exploitation 92
Steer, A. 27
Stern, M. J. 85
Stone, Moren Tibabo 22
sustainability 27–8, 40, 48, 51, 72–3
Sustainable Development Goals, UN 1
Sustainable Livelihood Framework (SLF) 27
sustainable marine-wildlife ecotourism 69–86
sustainable tourism 24
Swanson, Jason R. 3
systems, defined 23
system thinking approach, in tourism 23–5, 41
Szteren, Diana 91

The International Ecotourism Society (TIES)
    72
Tilden, F. 72, 86
Tonga Whale Guide Training Program
    (TWGTP) 71, 76–8, 86
Torra Conservancy, in Namibia 58
tour guides see guides
tourism: activities on farm 17; in Cuba 7;
    earnings through 36–7; impacts to farm 16;
    industry 24; leakages from 49–50, 50;
    protected areas (PAs) and 22–3; public
    funding for 39; as sensitive business 35; and
    socio-economic development in southern
    Africa 47–64; souvenir sales 17; spiralling
    up effect, creating 16; sustainable 24; on
    systems thinking 24, 41; see also ecotourism
transformative tourism 73–4, 85, 86

United Nations: International Year of
    Sustainable Tourism Development 1;
    Sustainable Development Goals 1
United States Agency for International
    Development (USAID) 32, 35
Uruguay, wildlife-watching tourism in 91–7;
    see also Cabo Polonio (Uruguay)

Value Model of Interpretation 74
van der Merwe, P. 49
visitors memories, of wildlife tourism 72

Walker, K. 69, 72, 74, 77
Wallerstein, N. 27
Weaver, D. B. 96
Weiler, B. 69, 73, 74, 77
whale ecotourism industry 70–1, 81
Wilderness Safaris (WS) 52–3; contributions to
    community development projects 59, 61;

contributions to environmental education programme 61, **61**; in infrastructure developments 59; payment of lease fees 58, **60**
wildlife ecotourism 69–70; in community 32–4
wildlife-watching tourism: in Cabo Polonio (Uruguay) 91–7

Wollenberg, E. 25
workforce nationalities **56**
World Wildlife Fund (WWF) 52

youth environmental education programmes 61

For Product Safety Concerns and Information please contact our EU
representative GPSR@taylorandfrancis.com
Taylor & Francis Verlag GmbH, Kaufingerstraße 24, 80331 München, Germany